# The Avatar® Path

## The Way We Came

by Harry Palmer

All our love to the people who contributed
to the creation of this book.

Cover art & layout by
Jim Becker

***Publisher's Note and Disclaimer:***
*The characters and events described in this book are intended
to entertain and teach rather than present an exact factual
history of real people or events.*

published by

Star's Edge International®
237 North Westmonte Drive
Altamonte Springs, Florida 32714
USA

The Avatar Path: The Way We Came

ISBN: 978-1-891575-68-6

# Table Of Contents

# BOOK II: SHAPING REALITY

## BOOK ĭĭĭ: ᛗARKETĭᏂG EᏂᏞĭᏂᏂTEᏂᛗEᏂT

Table Of Contents

### About the title of this book.

THE WAY WE CAME is **about** a self-evolvement journey to higher awareness. In terms of doingness, it begins with imitating, evolves to exploring, and culminates in creating. In terms of beingness, it begins with identity, evolves to "I am," and culminates in Source Being.

The AVATAR PATH is a breadcrumb trail of human potential courses for anyone who wishes to accelerate his or her own evolvement to higher awareness.

# Prologue

Like most journeys, self-evolvement has a starting point. That starting point is the recognition that some (or even most) of your guiding values and beliefs are based on imitation of parents, teachers, peers, satisfied customers, celebrities, authorities, the successful, or even the world's failures.

The life you are living is a copy of someone else's. It is a patchwork quilt of borrowings and unconscious influences. When you recognize this, really see it, something independent of any mental embellishment awakens—a new self. You can call this new self, "I am." This ineffable spirit— authentic YOU—wakes up with a desire to explore its potential.

*ineffable:* incapable of being expressed in words.

The articles and stories in the pages that follow are intended to illuminate archetypes in consciousness that will assist your growth. As you read, several things will happen: the expectations and opinions of others will be recognized and re-considered; personal values will be re-examined; and patterns of behaviors will change. And most importantly, YOU, that ineffable explorer, will begin awakening as a Source Being. This is a heroic journey.

Avatar.

The only provisions you need are courage, honesty, and perseverance. If people or circumstances have conspired to convince you that you lack these supplies, caches have been left along the way for you to find.

Right up front, I'll tell you a secret. As secrets go, this one is in the top ten. If it doesn't ring true for you right now, that's okay. Part of this journey is recovering the viewpoint that recognizes the truth of this powerful secret. The secret is nothing can harm a Source Being.

This isn't an easy truth to accept. The universe's position is that it can roll over you, grind your flesh up, or incinerate your consciousness any time it pleases. It can visit pain and suffering, or pleasure and happiness at its whim. It can snuff out your life unexpectedly. At any moment it can humble you into insignificance by its awesome magnificence. And always it demands that you follow certain of its rules or perish.

But what perishes? You are not a meat body. You are not thoughts. No thought or word can describe you. Thoughts and words are concepts and you are not a concept. You are not anything that can be named. What are you?

The universe can be broadly described in terms of matter, energy, space, and time, but you are not any of these. All definitions and descriptions are part of the universe. You are part of... well that's the question, isn't it?

# Book I:
## Solid
## Foundations

# THE STORY OF THE AVATAR MATERIALS

Eastern techniques of meditation describe four stages of mental engagements:

The first is forcible engagement. This 'mounts' the mind or directs the mind at some object.

The second is interrupted mental engagement. This is the process of noticing, stop noticing, and then noticing again in greater detail.

The third is uninterrupted engagement of the mind, which is concentration.

The fourth is a spontaneous engagement of the mind on a connection that just appeared. Ah ha!

Realizations (or insights) are spontaneous engagements of the mind.

*One of the abilities that you can profitably improve is directing your attention. If you have not done the Basic Attention Management Mini-Course, it is recommended. It will increase the amount of free attention that is available to you by recovering attention that you have misplaced or abandoned.*

*Visit www.TheAvatarCourse.com/attention for a free download of this mini-course.*

Chapter I

# Hunting Realizations

Realization is the *experience* of moving from a fixed viewpoint on a subject or event into a broader more understanding viewpoint. It is the moment in which something perplexing is worked out; it is a pleasant shock, a light penetrating the darkness, a discovery, the revelation of a solution. It's a moment of epiphany, an insight. "I just realized I was dreaming," or "I just realized that it wasn't my mother's fault." Realizations are the building blocks of self-evolvement, each one you have is a step toward greater wisdom and freedom.

Realizations may arrive gradually like the morning dawn, or suddenly like flashes of lightening; some take years of study to fully reveal themselves, others are instantly *gobsmacking* (shocking, surprising). Realizations are unique experiences—

world lessons. They are the keys and combinations that specifically unlock the reasons behind your thinking and being.

Someone else's realization may be interesting or educational, but they will not sort out or tame the mental territory that is uniquely yours. Your own realizations are more than insights, more than words; they are a release of transforming and restorative energy, a sigh of relief.

Stories can trigger realizations—not so much by the data conveyed in the story as by the personal connection that you make with the story. The classic Indian story of blind men describing an elephant illustrates this personal connection: the blind man who feels a leg says the elephant is like a pillar; the one who feels the tail says the elephant is like a rope; the one who feels the trunk says the elephant is like a tree branch; the one who feels the ear says the elephant is like a hand fan; the one who feels the belly says the elephant is like a wall; and the one who feels the tusk says the elephant is like a solid pipe. Realizations only occur within the framework of your own reality.

Preconceptions and assertions prevent realizations. Sometimes the action of pursuing other people's attention or admiration conflicts with the vulnerability required for facing something unknown. Posturing and striving for recognition have stunted the personal growth of more than a few—realizing for the applause of an audience creates stress rather than relief. It can be frightening to examine something without a prepared answer, to look without already knowing, but the rewards are priceless realizations.

Realizations result in beneficial changes in your health, your relationships, and your perspectives of life. Realizations give rise to qualities like responsibility, maturity, compassion, tolerance, patience, discernment, and confidence.

Your progress toward higher awareness can be measured by the number of honest realizations you have. Things begin (or cease) to make sense, horizons expand, and there is a pattern to events. The possibility of steering your own life and living deliberately becomes real. Hidden influences are dissolved into light.

So OK, realizations are good things. Where do they come from and how do you find them?

Realizations reside in the unknowns and misunderstandings of consciousness. An unknown is something that isn't recognized—an event, a person, a connection, or a condition, i.e., a missing piece. A misunderstanding is a failure to interpret something correctly. Making known what was previously unknown, or correcting something that was previously misunderstood, are the processes that result in realizations. *Oh hey, I know what that is. I see it now.*

Realizations happen in the safety of a friendly environment or in moments of reflective solitude. (They are slow to appear when being vulnerable is dangerous.) Surrendering one's attachment to right and wrong brings a fresh clarity; respecting differences in viewpoints loosens the grip of unawareness, and practicing compassion and reverence deepens one's insights.

Sadly, some will only deal in the realizations of others, written neatly in books of doctrine. It is easier than risking the humiliation of being singled out. Stay with the herd. Follow the examples. Sacrifice your own discoveries for the praise of being able to parrot someone else's thoughts. This is the path of self-solidification, not self-evolvement.

So the first step of hunting realizations is mustering your courage. You may have to look into places that you would rather not.

## Three-Ticket-Special

One summer, when I was a kid, we went to the county fair. (I grew up in rural Pennsylvania where there was no TV, no crowds, just tractors and cows.) So twenty acres of tents, and shooting galleries, and sideshows—not to mention a Ferris wheel, a dozen carnival rides, and a noisy, brightly lit midway— was about the most open-mouthed excitement I had experienced.

At the very end of the midway was an attraction called the Haunted Castle of Horrors. The barker's spiel promised: *frightening sights beyond human imagination, inhuman oddities, bloodthirsty apparitions, enter at your own risk.* On either side of the castle's entrance were two twenty-foot oil paintings on hanging canvases, depicting two passenger trains, loaded with zombies, about to collide.

*Tickets only a dime, one thin dime.* At the ticket window it was another story. Tickets were three for a quarter. *Step right up, sonny, three trips that you will never forget and only two bits.* Hoping he wouldn't recognize me for a hayseed, I fished another dime and nickel out of my hand-me-down coveralls.

I stood in front of the castle door listening to the shrieks and noises from inside. My knees were trembling and my steps shortened to about an inch. A rough shove, and I was through the door into a narrow, dark hallway. Around the first corner was a torture scene of a skeleton being stretched on a rack; rats huddled near by. The floor started shaking and a blast of air that smelled like old inner tubes hit me in the face. I stumbled on.

Around the next corner, a door slammed behind me. In the dim lights, I could see that I was standing between railroad tracks. Suddenly a train horn blew, a bell began ringing, and what looked like the headlight of a train appeared ahead of me. To the right and left were walls and I couldn't go back; I was trapped. The train noises grew louder and faster, and then the ghost train passed right through me (or so it seemed) leaving flashes of coach windows on the walls.

Around another corner, it felt like I was walking on sponges. I kept moving as fast as I could, hurrying past several rooms of stuffed animals, mummies in coffins, and macabre execution scenes. Jarring sounds: fingernails scraping a chalkboard, pebbles rattling in a pail—I covered my ears and ran.

Finally a huge, whirling, black-and-white hypnotic disk, which seemed to draw me forward, appeared, and a door opened. I was back out in the glare of the midway, mouth open, white as a sheet.

How long until customers used the second ticket depended upon how frightened they were. It took me over an hour, and for some, I imagined, they would never return. I walked up the crowded midway, watched a man win a teddy bear for his girl friend, checked out the Four-H sausage concession, and strolled through a poultry tent of blue-ribbon winners. Finally, trying to appear to be just wandering casually, I was back in front of the Haunted Castle of Horrors.

The second time through I paid more attention. I took the rattles and shakes and loud noises less personally. It wasn't as if anyone was trying to scare me, they were just trying to be scary. I started to relax, took second looks at things, and even enjoyed myself. This time when I stepped back on the midway, I had been entertained and was smiling.

*Consciousness thinks; awareness watches.*

Ten minutes and a funnel cake later I cashed in the third ticket. On this trip I took my time. I studied the costumed mannequins without fear. I noticed things I had not noticed before; some of the stuffed animals were the worse for the wear, rips and patches of hair were missing. I studied how the displays worked, and even peeked behind the scenes. In the end, I realized that the only reason anything in the Haunted Castle of Horrors was scary was because I expected it to be scary. In reality, it was just a moderately sized trailer, sectioned off with plywood walls, behind a tip-up front painted to look like a castle.

The point that I am making is that when you go hunting for realizations about why your life is the way it is, or what you could do to improve it, buy the three-ticket-special.

Avatar
Professional
Course students.
Orlando, FL,
October 2009

# THE STORY OF
# THE AVATAR MATERIALS

### Awareness and Consciousness

Awareness and consciousness are not the same.

Awareness is beyond description. The closest analogy to awareness is space. Awareness is the fuel that powers consciousness.

Awareness of something by something, within a span of time, is consciousness. Consciousness is subject to change, awareness is not.

# THE STORY OF
# THE AVATAR MATERIALS

Consciousness is a dial, not a switch.

Life is so incredibly rich with stimulus and phenomena that we need to generalize this richness to a manageable level. Usually we think of consciousness as a tool that allows us to become brighter, and more discerning, but it is also a tool for dumbing-us-down.

Life is so beautifully complex that unless we dumb ourselves down, we are just overwhelmed by the experience. Every moment is different in some way from every other moment. Every leaf, every snowflake, every grain of sand in the universe is unique. Every breath you take is different in some way from the breath before it. Every second that you experience is different in a million ways from the second that preceded it. This moment is different from every other moment in your life. When people become aware of this, everything stops, and you begin hearing responses like "awesome, unbelievable, wow."

People go to school to dumb down, and when they go long enough, they earn a degree. Maybe it will say Bachelors degree, but what it should say is now-dumb-enough-to-mistake-similarity-in-things-that-are-uniquely-different.

*Science can demonstrate that certain physical character-
istics are genetically encoded in an individual's DNA.
One person's blue eyes and another's brown eyes can
be traced to certain genetic configurations. Skin, scales,
feathers, and hair, as well as thousands of other physical
traits, can be explained in terms of inherited genetic
material, but what about instincts, social behaviors, and
humanitarian motives? Where do they come from?*

Chapter 2

# Before The Ash Falls

I used to raise pigs and observed that they were
naturally adept at building shelters. That's probably where the story of "The Three Little Pigs" comes
from. The first little pig built his house of straw, the
second little pig built his house of sticks, and the
third little pig built his house of bricks. That last
construction may have been creative license on the
part of the storyteller, but pigs really do build
shelters, and they are quite good at it.

I had a 300-pound sow named Violet who could
turn a soft piece of ground and a brush pile into a
pig shelter in an amazingly short time. She was a
regular beaver. She would drag branches together
into a pile, dump mouthfuls of sod on them, and
then roll the pile flat. Then she would drag on a
few more branches, more mouthfuls of sod, and

then roll it flat again. At first I thought she was building a foundation, which really would have been surprising. Foundations are a sign that a consciousness has awakened that can predict consequences. If you are working on an archeological excavation, searching for ancient civilizations, and you discover something that looks like a foundation, you have hit pay dirt. Foundations are a crossover from instinctive shelter building to intelligent shelter building. (This same crossover exists in the construction of lives.)

Anyhow, the pig wasn't building a foundation; she was building a shelter from the top down. The matted pile of sticks and sod was her roof. Once it satisfied her, she lifted the edge with her nose and crawled under. Then she stood up and the roof bent to the curve of her back. From the underside she pushed up a dirt wall with her snout. When the dirt around her was a foot high, she knelt down in the hole she had excavated and let the dome roof rest on the dirt. I wondered if this was the natural archetype for cathedrals and capitol buildings. It is humbling to think that the U.S. Capitol building may have been modeled after a pig shelter.

There was no exit. At first, I thought this was a mistake, but on second thought, if you are giving birth to a dozen lively baby pigs (which she did a few hours later) you could appreciate her design.

In a matter of one afternoon, Violet had built a one-pig dome with a matted waterproof roof that would protect her new family from late spring snows. Some pig! What intrigued me was that Violet had been born and raised on a concrete floor in a commercial pig farm. How did she know about building shelters?

Baby pigs are vulnerable to cold, and without knowledge of shelters the species could not survive. So how is this shelter-building instinct passed from generation to generation? I'm sure that the width of her snout and the color of her eyes were determined by inherited DNA, but where did she inherit her knowledge of shelters? Is shelter building an evolved behavior developed over many generations and reinforced by natural selection?

Watching Violet build her house left me wondering if there is some cosmic, consciousness memory bank that passes instincts from generation to generation, species to species, some sort of "between lives" storage area.

Of course, instincts can limit you to an outmoded behavior. (Probably why intelligence was invented, duh!) Following instincts is about as conservative as you can get. If something worked for granddad, then it will work for you. Maybe... maybe, as long as the challenges faced by your granddad were the same ones that are confronting you.

If the climate became warmer, would Violet still build a shelter for her piglets? Would they suffocate in the heat? I personally think Violet would outvote her instincts and intelligently figure something out. But it does raise serious questions for species with limited intelligence. And what if the dirt becomes poisoned from pollution or fallout? Decontamination is probably beyond a pig's intelligence.

## Simple Answers

At the urging of some hippie friends, I went to visit an interesting fellow that lived in a converted milk house attached to cinder block barn. He was a welder, and wore a welding helmet that he could tip into place with a nod of his head, and a rust-stained, ankle-length leather apron over his coveralls. The helmet was large, but even so, there were singed areas in his gray beard where sparks had landed.

The barn was a studio where he hammered and welded wrought iron patio furniture. He was locally famous for his ironwork. He also was a poet, had spent a year in prison, and had lived many years as a monk in India. He made no claims, but the consensus opinion of my friends was that he had found enlightenment.

After a handshake and an exchange of first names, he put me to work with a, "put these there." For the next twenty minutes I loaded the 'these' (enamel sprayed iron chairs) into the 'there' of a U-Haul trailer.

When I was finished he turned off his torch with a pop and tipped back his welding helmet. "Can you run a power sander?" he asked.

Since I had not come to apply for a job, I just jumped right in and asked him, "How do you find enlightenment?"

"Turn off your television, throw away your books, and be yourself," he said. And then pointed, "The sander is in the corner." A nod and his welding helmet tipped back into place.

In the sixties, I dropped out and returned to the land. The plan was to be self-sufficient: to grow my own food, build my own house, and survive by my own efforts.

You want to know something? Living off the land was the easiest thing I ever did. All the problems of what to grow, when to plant, and how to build, were solved hundreds of years ago. I had a house, plenty to eat, and was bored almost to death. Instead of surviving, I felt like I was on a path to extinction. Thriving does not always mean you are evolving. When you get down to it, evolving seems more important than thriving. So maybe the challenges we face are good things.

I used to end my talks with a story about a tropical rodent that evolved during the age of the dinosaur. This little quadruped was unique because it was covered with thin, single-quill feathers that you and I would call hair.

Hair in a tropical climate is not a good idea; it doesn't really solve any environmental problem. In fact, it is a liability. So much so that the poor creature had to burrow underground, and only come out at night. On the plus side, it did avoid cold-blooded predators that hunted in the heat of the day.

But fashion-wise, the time was all scales and thick hide. Hair was an oddity. It's not hard to imagine the great scaly rulers of the Jurassic swamps looking at the hairy rodent burrowing in the ground and hear them laughing. Hair! Living underground! What a freak!

Then it started to snow!

Of course, you know the rest of the story: Rodents survived the ice age, dinosaurs didn't.

Growing hair was pre-adaptive evolution. It didn't come from instincts, or even from intelligence; it was a mutation. Call it dumb luck if you want to, but having hair and a burrowing ability prepared the ancestor of the mouse family for the future. If there is some fund of collective consciousness that dutifully records the experiences of life, and designs instincts for the next generation, this mouse started a new chapter. Fur was a serendipitous mutation that illustrates that sometimes you survive by being different and breaking with the past.

The more self-designing that a creature becomes, the more it can adapt to changes. If the dinosaur had greater intelligence and fewer instincts, it might have survived the Ice Age wearing a mouse-skin coat, but the dinosaur was not self-designing; it lacked the intelligence and flexibility to manage major changes.

Today, tens of thousands of Avatar students are self-designing foundations that will pre-adapt them for the social change that is beginning: The crossover point from mutually destructive societies to an enlightened planetary civilization. You could say that Avatars are growing hair. In this case, hair is the ability to live deliberately and see others compassionately, the ability to trust and act honestly, the ability to listen and share, and the ability to predict and shape future realities.

While a few scaly skeptics are laughing, pointing fingers and yelling, "Cult!", the ash is beginning to fall.

*Recognizing good advice is not the same as experiencing. Recognizing will cause you to nod, but experiencing will teach you to duck.*

# THE STORY OF
# THE AVATAR MATERIALS

### What are Avatars told to believe?

The Avatar Materials produce profound increases in self-awareness. This inspires graduates to make changes in their values and goals. These changes are always self-determined and are not the result of any deliberate influence or persuasion by the teacher. Avatar Masters are discouraged from passing their own beliefs to students.

*In a graduation commencement address given on April 28, 1990, in Nice, France, Harry made it clear what he expected from Avatar Masters:*

Anyone can decide their beliefs are righteous. Any belief can be dressed up to look righteous. Righteous beliefs are inscribed upon parchment and in holy books. Eventually they become slogans on battle flags and are used to justify insensitive acts for which no sane individual would ever assume personal responsibility. If they did, they would be tried and convicted for murder. So people die by the thousands with righteous beliefs on every side.

It is better that you denounce Avatar a thousand times than use it even once as a righteous belief to justify your actions. Champion no cause above personal responsibility.

*I'd like to be remembered as more
of a pointer than an explainer.*

Chapter 3

# Explanations

Ask people what they believe and you are likely
to get an assortment of what they want, what they
have heard, what sounds reasonable, or what is
most likely to be praised.

Do they believe the things that they are assert-
ing? Most of the time the answer is no. But digging
beneath the asserted beliefs we find the real beliefs
that are shaping behavior and creating reality.

The real beliefs, whether deliberately chosen or
methodically indoctrinated, create a blueprint for
what we perceive and how we interpret it. They
are the foundation of our life. During ordinary
moments of consciousness this blueprint causes us
to perceive certain things, and to tune out certain
other things. Changing a real belief can change our
future, can change what we pay attention to, and
can change what we see. A real belief can actually
make objects disappear from our consideration.

*What you
believe you
should believe
is a real belief.*

A stage magician hypnotized a subject and asked
him to remove his shoes. He did. The hypnotist

then installed a real belief (he called it a post-hypnotic suggestion) so that when the subject awoke he would not see his shoes. The shoes were then placed on the floor, in plain sight, a few feet in front of the subject's chair.

The hypnotist counted backwards from five to one; telling the subject between each number that he was gradually awakening and would on the count of one, fully awaken, feeling happy and refreshed.

The subject awoke smiling as if nothing had occurred. "I'm sorry," he said, "I guess I'm not a very good subject."

The hypnotist pointed at the subject's feet and asked, "Where are your shoes?"

For an instant the subject was baffled that his shoes were missing. He looked around; looked right past the shoes in plain sight, and finally replied that he had not worn any shoes.

The hypnotist pressed him. "Do you mean to tell me that you came to the theater tonight without any shoes?"

The audience laughed and the subject began to squirm and become defensive. "Yes," he said, "I do that all the time!"

"You come to the theater without shoes?"

"It is my way of protesting," asserted the subject.

"May I ask, what are you protesting?" asked the hypnotist.

"I'm protesting a system that forces me to do things that I don't want to do," he asserted.

"And you don't want to wear shoes?" asked the hypnotist.

"That's right."

*If you push a mind for an answer, it will awaken imagination to present one.*

The hypnotist then pointed directly at the shoes, touched them, and tapped them on the floor. "Aren't these your shoes?"

The subject stared for several seconds; his mind began to register the shoes in front of him, and further to register that the shoes were his.

"Oh yeah, I must have taken them off when I came on stage so I wouldn't fall. They are new and the bottoms are still slippery."

What is truly remarkable about this event is that the hypnotist's implanted belief not only caused the shoes to disappear from the man's perception, but also led the man to create a reasonable explanation for the missing shoes.

Of course, the reasonable explanation was not the real cause of the experience. The reasonable explanation was an asserted belief created after the fact. The real cause of the experience was some approximation of the hypnotist's suggested belief: "When you awaken, you will not be able to see your shoes even though they are right in front of you."

A transparent belief, hypnotically implanted, can create a mental blueprint that causes the mind to selectively perceive.

The prime directive of the mind, its *raison d'etre*, is to explain what is perceived. In this case, it not only created an explanation but also embellished upon it with a new belief created out of thin air: "I'm protesting a system that forces me to do things that I don't want to do."

Why didn't the subject just say, "I don't know where my shoes are?" That would have been an honest answer, but it would have forced his mind into a vulnerable state of not knowing. Not knowing can be humiliating as well as dangerous. A common response to not knowing is to engage in speculations, assumptions, and... explanations!

*The mind has a deep compelling urge to be right, and this urge can cause people to assert things that they really don't believe.*

Some psychoanalysts will tell us that explaining is a defense mechanism: A means of avoiding a potential threat to self-esteem or a conflict with self-image. It is a mind suffering from incomplete data and engaging its own imagination to make itself right and protect self-esteem. People do not easily tolerate a state of not knowing, and often choose to distort reality rather than suffer vulnerability. That is the path our hypnotized subject followed.

Our subject was compensating for incomplete data caused by a particular kind of implanted belief, but similar defense mechanisms can be found for all sorts of transparent beliefs. The mind has a deep compelling urge to be right, and this urge can cause us to assert things that we did not intentionally set out to believe. This complicates what would otherwise be a clear connection between our beliefs and our experiences.

# THE STORY OF
# THE AVATAR MATERIALS

### What is personal responsibility?

Personal responsibility is the ability to determine one's own decisions, choices, and actions. In Avatar, this is called being source. A natural outcome of increasing this ability is that people discover areas in their lives that they haven't been controlling.

A fundamental characteristic of people who support the creation of an enlightened planetary civilization is a high level of personal responsibility.

# The Story of
# The Avatar Materials

### What is a belief?

A belief is an expression that exhibits a degree of conviction or certainty.

It is a verbal or non-verbal representation of one or more of the following: an expectation *(this is going to be difficult)*, an opinion or assumption *(this is difficult)*, or an interpretation *(it's difficult because it's hard to accept)*.

*There are at least two categories of identities. The first are **role identities**, which are deliberately created and exist only for as long as you create them, and second are **persistent identities**, which exist continually, exactly as they were unconsciously created in some past moment.*

Chapter 4

# Two Types Of Identities

Have you ever heard someone say, "Just who do you think you are?"

The presumed intention of the speaker is to communicate to someone that they have somehow become confused and aren't who they think they are. "Just who do you think you are?" It is not so much a question as it is a statement. It is often followed by an unkindly appraisal such as, "I'll tell you who you are...."

Abusive intent aside, the speaker has at least a dim comprehension that identities have more to do with thoughts, ideas, and beliefs (mental concepts) than with physical appearances. And in that respect, he or she has communicated an important truth. Who you think you are is *an identity.*

There are at least two categories of identities. The first are **role identities**, which are *deliberately* created and exist only for as long as you create

*One of our most highly developed mental abilities is pretending to be something that we are not.*

**model:** to base something, especially one's appearance or behavior, on somebody else.

them. These are copies of behaviors and appearances from people that you like or admire. For the most part, role identities, even after they become habitual, can be self-modified. Most people have many role identities: *Rich man, poor man, beggar man, thief. Doctor, lawyer, Indian chief.*

When you wish to be recognized, you assume one of these role identities; it is like presenting a business card. The role identity you assume may be exactly like one you assumed in the past, giving the impression of continuity, and allowing recognition and prediction by others. "Oh, it's Frank, the postman."

One day you assume an entirely new identity, (you can have many, remember), which you create (model) according to a different archetype, e.g. truckdriver, TV repairman, car salesman. Each new role identity sends the message that you have changed, at least superficially, which is likely to draw from certain people the response: "Who do you think you are?"

This is another way of saying: "Will you please go back to creating yourself the way you were." Some times a plan for personal growth will come into conflict with someone who doesn't want you to change.

**default:** an option that will automatically be selected if a person doesn't choose one.

The second category of identity is **persistent identities**, which exist, with only slight modifications, exactly as they were created in some past *moment of conflict.* Persistent identities are unconsciously modeled after people you disliked or resisted, and, well, persistent identities persist.

Persistent identities are what you display when you are not deliberately displaying created role identities. You could call them the default identities. They are triggered by your thoughts, the environment, or other people. They seem to be independent of your control, leading some people to mistakenly consider them the real self. *That's just the way I am.* Of course, that is a lie, real self is not like anything.

Because persistent identities were modeled after an opponent during a moment of conflict, they have two principle aspects: first is a model of the opponent (I am like my opponent), second is a model of someone who would be the opposite of the opponent (I am not like my opponent). When a persistent identity is triggered, only one of the aspects is displayed—either the opponent identity or someone who would oppose the opponent identity. A persistent identity has an iceberg quality about it in that only half of it appears at a time. For example, *Fred* is an identity, and so too is *not-like-Fred*. Fred and not-like-Fred are parts of one mental construction held together by conflict.

Role identities and persistent identities, these two categories of identities, although acquired in very different ways—the first the product of desire, the second the product of resistance—still function similarily: They both act as filters and interpreters; they both set standards for what is right or wrong,

good or bad; they both determine values, abilities, and goals; and they both affect the character of a person's internal monologue. An identity is second only to a belief in regard to the influence it has on a person's life.

The different identities that you assume (or that consume you) generate different considerations. Your warrior identity probably has different standards than your holy man identity, and your mother identity probably has different standards than your professional identity. You might welcome an experience in one identity yet resist the same experience in a different identity. This gives rise to the often heard statement, "I have to be in the mood."

At one time or another, most people have experienced internal conflicts as the result of shifting identities. The addict is a stark example of this. He or she wakes up after a hard-party-night and the morning role identity says, "That's it, I'm never going to do that again." Some hours later a persistent evening identity takes over and says, "Life is short, so let's party." The internal conflict causes life to spin out of control; the toughest battles are between "who-I-want-to-be" and "who-I-can't help-being."

Certain identities favor certain emotional responses. Other identities influence what you consider is real, and what you consider is illusion. Identities influence what you perceive, and what you ignore. For example, a barber notices haircuts, a policeman notices suspicious behavior, and an architect notices buildings.

Identities open and close possibilities, and determine achievement. Also they influence the structure and health of the physical body, and the degree of ease or stress caused by different people and environments. Identities influence our interpretation of incoming impressions as well as our outgoing actions and reactions.

Deliberately chosen role identities can enhance your life, but uncontrolled persistent identities can sabotage everything.

Before the Avatar Materials appeared on the scene, there was a great variance from person to person, and from technique to technique, as to how much, if any, persistent identities could be modified. Most people could be trained (or train themselves) into role identities. Colleges and universities turned out doctors, lawyers, and engineers; charm schools turned out hostesses and entertainers; public schools turned out socially responsible citizens. These were all role identities.

**resistance:** *opposition to changing one's viewpoint.*

Compulsive, destructive behaviors of persistent identities were excused as bad nurturing or a weakness in character. Preachers and superstitious moralists talked about evil. Only a perceptive and patient few saw the source of destructive behavior for what it was, a misunderstood functioning of consciousness—an antiquated instinct to mentally duplicate, and unconsciously store, experiences involving conflict.

**discreate:** *the non-action of ceasing to create.*

Persistent identities led some to assume (mistakenly) that people had a core personality that could not be changed. Leaders of the human potential movement were the first to realize that a person's core self—YOU—was undefinable and only acted through an identity. That meant, that by some event or circumstance a persistent identity was the conclusion of an experience rather than genetics. These same people realized that discovering a process to remove persistent identities could change the world.

But the mental slate of persistent identities was not easy to erase.

Many self-improvement seminars and workshops were (and still are) based on empowering successful role identities. The goal was for a specific role identity to become so habitual that it overwrote the influence of any persistent identities. Results were, unfortunately, temporary.

In some cases the seminar-empowered role identity made matters worse by creating an inner conflict between an *idealized self* and the *self one experiences*—who you want to be versus who you can't help being. This conflict of identities led to a loss of self-confidence, self-esteem, and self-respect.

So some people quietly took their meds, or clung to their enablers, or spent more money on more therapy, hoping or pretending they had modified their persistent identities. Socially, for approval or advantage, some displayed new behaviors publically, but the pretense was exhausting, and privately nothing had really changed other than their new preference for solitude.

Persistent identities seemed etched in mental steel. The good news is that they only *seemed* that way. What the Avatar Materials recognized was that a persistent identity was only showing the visible half of a polarized mental structure separated by a strong emotional charge. In 1991, a process was developed for integrating the resistance, and discreating both halves of a persistent identity.

(Today the Persistent Identity Process is successfully employed by thousands of Avatar Masters.)

# THE STORY OF
# THE AVATAR MATERIALS

**How does Avatar differ from other practices or self-help technologies?**

People usually argue for or against beliefs about what is true. They practice something because they believe it is true. Someone says, "This is the way to live," and because they are convincing, or a charismatic role model, or have some power over you, you believe their instructions. I'm not saying that this is necessarily a bad thing, but it is the big difference between Avatar and most other practices. Avatar is not going to tell you what to believe. It *will* reveal to you what you already believe and *why*.

Avatar will show you how to connect the dots between what you are believing and what you are experiencing in life, and it will teach you how to dissolve a belief that is creating an experience that you don't prefer. The focus is on exploring consciousness and only changing the things in life that you want to change.

Chapter 5

# Manageable Causes Versus Plausible Excuses

I've been noting the difference between manageable causes (something we can do something about) and plausible excuses (an excuse that is believable). I'm not a big fan of thinking backwards into the past, but sometimes a little of it is necessary. The strategy that I favor is to identify a situation, either good or bad, and examine the actions or inactions that were responsible for it. The actions that I'm particularly interested in are those that I can deliberately repeat, or those I can change, or those I can avoid doing in the future. These are manageable causes; I can manage them. Of course there may be unique circumstances or events that can't be managed, which also contribute to the situation: acts of God, difficult people, broken beyond repair, or used up. It's good to be able to recognize these so I can avoid making future plans that count on them.

*past:* a period of time which only exists in memory.

*situation:* a non-optimum condition.

The best argument for studying the past is to learn to repeat manageable actions that lead to favorable circumstances in the future. Or avoid manageable actions that are likely to lead to situations in the future. It is not a perfect system, but it does turn the odds in your favor.

Did you ever have one of those realizations where you pull a string on some situation and it just completely unravels back to some manageable cause? You go, "Yeah! Oh, yeah! YEAH!" You just learned something. Recognizing causes is the beginning of practical knowledge. Of the causes that contribute to a situation, some are easily managed, some require skill and training to manage, and some are apparently unmanageable.

Sometimes people get wrapped up in a situation and worry, explain, or blame. This is a mistake. Their efforts would be better spent on honestly discovering the manageable causes that are contributing to the creation of the situation. Working a problem means discovering manageable causes and then managing them!

*manageable:* capable of being governed, controlled, or guided.

*cause:* that upon which something (an effect) depends.

*plausible:* worthy of acceptance or approval.

A plausible excuse conveys the message that you are not at fault, because you couldn't do anything about it. NOT AT FAULT is the operative message. A plausible excuse is a claim that there are no **manageable** causes that contributed to the situation you are in. It is an attempt to avoid responsibility. The excuse is effective to the degree that you can get other people to agree with your helplessness.

Remember the best excuses you used in school? They always communicated something like this: "I really couldn't do anything about it, because..." And then you plugged in your favorite limitation, for example, "...because I didn't have time." As you grew more adept at excusing yourself, you filled in the blank with more customized limitations that the teacher would accept.

"I didn't get my homework done, because... teachers do not get paid enough!"

The word "excuse" comes from **ex** meaning "free" from and **cusa** meaning "cause." So the message behind an excuse is, "I was not cause!" And if you decide you were not cause, chances are good that you are a helpless effect.

Richard Bach, an American author, wrote, "Argue for your limitations, and sure enough they're yours." He could just as well have written, "Decide that you are helpless enough times, and you will be."

Remember when you explained to the teacher that you were late because you didn't wake up, and she replied that you were responsible because you didn't set an alarm clock? I'll bet you never used that excuse again. No good. It didn't free you from cause. Next time you'll be smarter and you'll know enough to say, "Because the wind-up alarm clock ran down in the middle of the night."

I tried this with a teacher once. Actually I used it three days in a row. The fourth time I tried to pull it, she opened the drawer of her desk and handed me an electric alarm clock. She just wasn't getting the message that there were no manageable causes that I could control to get to school on time. So I did what any healthy fifteen-year-old would do, I told the teacher I was sick!

Being sick is among the best excuses. Man, you can hammer that beauty home, and whole crowds of people will gather around and shout, "He can't do anything about it. He is sick!" And sure enough...

Being sick is an excuse that almost anyone will agree with. It is a beauty. It has to be at least part of the reason for the success of the medical profession. What a profession! They give you drugs to handle the discomforts caused by using the world's best excuse. And now you are really covered. "Sorry, I'm on medication." "Sorry, I'm under a doctor's care." It doesn't get more helpless than that.

Forgive my cynicism, but on this planet if you provide a service that validates a person's excuses, you are almost sure to be a success.

The world's best excuse is a note from the doctor. It is three times better than a note from the school nurse. And it is ten times better than a note from your mother, especially if you wrote it yourself.

Twenty years later, working on a sinus infection, I suddenly remembered the alarm clock episode and experienced a near-instant cure. This was one of those "Oh!" realizations: Coax someone toward responsibility and they get better; accept their excuses and they get sicker.

*Everyone has a right to choose what they believe, but no one is right because of what they believe. How we behave toward each other is the measure of right and wrong, not what we believe.*

If you are having a problem getting people to accept your excuses you have to learn to make them more overwhelming. Play with words like "unavoidable," "tragedy," "fate," or "God's will." No one is going to challenge those. Isn't that what fate means? "No one can do anything about it." God's will is the ultimate excuse.

Go ahead; try it. "I'm late because of... (lower your eyes and throw in a limp for good measure) unavoidable fate!" You see how helpless that is; no one is even going to try to get you to look for a manageable cause. Only a fool would challenge fate.

A plausible excuse has some other benefits. The person you give it to should still approve of you even though the situation-you-didn't-have-anything-to-do-with was a disaster. It just didn't turn out according to plan. Bad luck! You are covered; you've got a plausible excuse. Anyone who hears it should still like you, maybe even offer some sympathy, and realize that you're just another helpless victim of fate!

Maybe we could create an official no-responsibility passport. The first page would say, "The Supreme Universal Council decrees that this individual is helpless and has no responsibility for the life situations he/she appears in." Don't laugh; it's a good idea. What a relief, a no-responsibility passport, an NRP. If you arrive late for school, you just pull out your NRP and have the teacher stamp it. Think of how much time it would save the world. And how much illness it would prevent. It could cut healthcare costs by half.

Here's another reason it is a good idea. Every new excuse a person has to dream up whittles away at their attention power. If someone accepts their excuse for one situation, it wouldn't be wise of them to use the same excuse for the next situation. (And there will be another situation because they are not learning.) So people are faced with frequently having to create new excuses. It is not a one-time deal. But with a no-responsibility passport, they have proof that they are helpless and the pressure is off.

I'm in favor of making life easier for those people who are determined to fail.

Have you ever wanted to harm someone? It's easy; just suggest a plausible excuse that they can use anytime. This is called enabling a disability. That will reduce their power in a hurry. They'll be helpless in a few weeks. It is easier than murdering them, although it may not be any kinder.

I was middle aged before I realized that the people who would not accept my excuses were my friends.

Too often it is easier to give an explanation for a difficult situation than confront your own actions that might have contributed to the situation. "I couldn't do anything about it, because..." Tough love; "...because you are deliberately creating yourself as a helpless loser."

An excuse is an attempt to deny that this is a cause-and-effect universe. We do something and it produces an effect. We forget to do something and it does not produce an effect. We drop something and it falls on the floor: cause and effect. Most of us would not drop a book, watch it hit the floor, and then say, "Not my fault, I can't do anything about gravity."

Gravity is a plausible excuse, but the manageable cause in the book dropping is that YOU let go of it.

Manageable causes are your share of responsibility for a situation. I know it is an ugly question, but if you want to get to the bottom of a complaint in a hurry, ask: "What did you do?" Most of what happens to us, and I'm trying to be gentle, is in one way or another, at least partly our responsibility.

It's easy to say: "Everything that happens to YOU is at least partly your responsibility." It's not so easy to say: "Everything that happens to ME is at least partly my responsibility." See the difference? And it is even more humbling when you look for MY manageable actions that are partly responsible for creating the problem. If your purpose is to succeed, you will find them. If your purpose is to look good, maybe get re-elected, you will stick with plausible excuses.

When my goal is to remedy some situation: unhappiness, loneliness, failure, exhaustion, or despair; the place to start is with MY manageable actions that are contributing, or have contributed, to that situation.

Do you know what I'm getting at? When we look for manageable actions we are looking for our share of responsibility for what we are experiencing. We are actually looking for what we can do (or not do) to change the experience. When we do this, we move beyond the need of plausible excuses.

# The Story of
# The Avatar Materials

*How does Avatar affect future generations?*

One of the goals of Avatar is to make people more aware, to remind them that their highest nature is nonviolent, and to increase the amount of compassion and cooperation on the planet.

If you fired an arrow, stopped it in its flight, and sighted along the arrow, you would see where it was going. If you stopped Avatar in flight and sighted along it, you would see that it is headed toward an enlightened planetary civilization. Every person who becomes an Avatar shifts the collective consciousness toward the goal of greater tolerance and understanding.

The hope of future generations is that we awaken a consciousness that is increasingly immune to irrationality and that values wisdom. Helping yourself with Avatar helps everyone else, including future generations. With Avatar everyone wins.

# THE STORY OF
# THE AVATAR MATERIALS

Avatar

### Four Point Strategy

1. Maintain a keen and ongoing familiarly with your current location and condition.

2. Have a worthwhile objective that you believe can be achieved.

3. Increase your effectiveness by recognizing and utilizing available resources.

4. Create and execute doable plans leading toward the objective.

*In the foregoing chapter, I made the following points:*
*EXCUSES are responsibility limiters (blame avoiders) that*
*convey the message that one is not at fault. The most accept-*
*able excuses are explanations that people will find plausible.*
*MANAGEABLE CAUSES are beliefs, thoughts, and actions*
*that you can do something about; you can control them.*

Chapter 6

# Finding Manageable Causes

A situation is a non-optimum condition. Unhappiness, loneliness, failure, exhaustion, and despair are typical personal situations. Also, so are being broke, being ill, or feeling overwhelmed. Also, so are not being the person you would like to be, and not doing the things that you would like to do.

Situations are usually the result of multiple causes. Think of a lake that is fed by multiple streams of water. It is true that some causes have a quality of fate, but other causes are manageable. And managing just one cause can affect an entire situation. If you focus on the "fated" causes, there is little that you can do other than continue to suffer and make plausible excuses. However, if you focus on finding the manageable causes and controlling them, you can change the situation.

What you believe is the most powerful contributing cause to any personal situation. Diet, health, influence of the environment, influence of associations, and habits may also be contributing causes to a situation, but each of them stands a good chance of being managed just by managing your beliefs. This is why the Avatar Materials are so valuable, they teach an effective belief management system.

If your life goes flat, you can blame fate or you can examine the situation (honestly) and look for manageable causes.

Now there is one very obvious thing you have to do in order to find a manageable cause. You have to look! You have to look at the situation you are in, realize it has multiple causes, and discover at least one cause that is manageable. You have to confront the situation as it is. That means developing an ability to set aside emotions, assumptions, expectations, and discouragement. These are skills honed early on in sections of the Avatar Materials.

For some people, the first response to a situation is assignment of blame. Who did it? ("I'm unhappy because Mommy was mean to me." Maybe that's true, but it is certainly not the only cause of their unhappiness.) What they are missing is that situations have multiple causes including predispositions. The same people may consider that a question has only one answer. This is very narrow- minded thinking, and inevitably causes situations to persist.

There is an instinctive temptation to protect oneself with excuses. It may be the fatal flaw of our species. To survive, successfully, you have to take control of this mental process, otherwise the mind will seek plausible excuses rather than manageable causes.

Avatar.

Here is how it works. Something has gone wrong in your life. Something didn't work out. You find yourself experiencing something other than an optimum state, something darker or even painful. Recognize, you have a situation. You can take the easy route, be a victim and blame it on someone else, or you can concentrate on discovering (and presumably changing) causes that you can control. Failing to find a cause you can manage is a recipe for continued suffering.

The only sound advice is don't give up. Look hard enough and long enough and you will find that there is something that you can do that will positively affect the situation that you are in.

Okay, time for some painful honesty. Ask yourself, am I looking for a manageable cause that I can control to resolve the situation, or am I looking for a plausible excuse that will confirm that it's not my fault? More often than not, you will find what you are motivated to find.

The next question, and this is really a whack on the side of the head, is: "Do you really want to resolve the situation?" If a situation serves you, you might not want to resolve it. It could be the excuse you are looking for to justify running away. It could be holding off something worse. It could be getting you extra attention or some goods and services. It could be something that you subconsciously feel that you deserve. We've all known people who get bailed out of a problem and go right out and create it all over again. Using your mind to keep you in trouble rather than solving your problems, is called self-sabotage. Self-sabotage afflicts more people than you might imagine, even entire nations.

Some prejudices are so fixed by repeated indoctrination or painful experiences that a person will just outright refuse to inspect them. The person's behavior will appear stupid or even bizarre. Take a close look at any hate group and you will find their thinking is severely flawed. Their common denominator is blame. They are unable or unwilling to find any manageable cause for why they feel like angry victims.... That would require personal responsibility. The thing they are most certain of is that the situation they are in is not their fault. They blame minorities, governments, or even extraterrestrials for their oppression. Their situation never resolves, and the causes they blame grow stronger.

When you examine a situation, your ability to admit that you don't already know cannot be overvalued. It allows you to look beyond fixed ideas and excuses and find a manageable cause that you can do something about. It takes a measure of courage to look without expectation, to trace something unpleasant back along its route of development, and to determine what step in that development you could be responsible for.

A big part of the Avatar training is teaching a spirit (you) how to operate a mind efficiently.

It's easy to become fixed on what you can't change, but that's not what you are looking for. You are looking for manageable causes. Finding them will determine whether you go through life making excuses for your problems or finding solutions. This lesson by itself is a major step in self-evolvement.

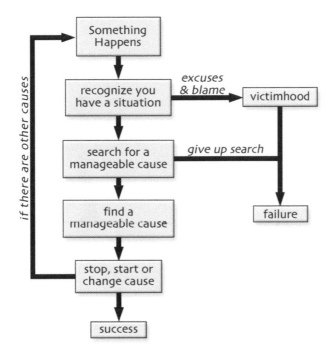

# THE STORY OF
# THE AVATAR MATERIALS

*I suspect the question you are asked most often is: "What is Avatar?" So, what is Avatar?*

Avatar is about every reality that is, was or will be. I know that's not very descriptive, but it is the truest statement I can make. Avatar deals with creation, which I define as anything that has definition or limits in space, time, or awareness. That covers the universe and everything in it.

Since most people are not really ready to engage Avatar at such an all-encompassing level, I usually talk about beliefs. People have an instinctive recognition that what they believe has a consequence on their lives. The principle dilemma of existence is what to believe. That's the philosophic abyss that confronts everyone. That's the abyss called: "I don't know." It's dangerous not to know. At the edge of this abyss are the shops of the belief peddlers. Some shops are lavish and hallowed with histories. Some are Volkswagen buses driven by cult recruiters. Everybody is selling a program and a one-way pass to the land of truth on the other side of the abyss. There are thousands of bridges across the abyss, and each one leads to a slightly different reality.

Of course, Avatar is there too, but what is different about Avatar is that the ticket is round trip!

Chapter 7

# Break Your Jug

There is an old story about a farmer who finds a pumpkin that has just started to develop. To protect the little pumpkin against the elements, he slips it inside a jug. Then he goes on his way and forgets about it. When harvest time comes, the pumpkin has grown only as large as the jug. The jug that once protected it, eventually limits its growth.

Many people are in the same situation as the pumpkin. To find protection, they have embraced sheltering beliefs about who they are, what they can do, and what they can become. For a time these beliefs offer comfort and protection, but beliefs, particularly limiting beliefs, soon lose their usefulness. Limiting beliefs form a jug. It is a person's own considerations that limit his or her potential. Once the "truth" of a limiting belief has been realized, a person stops growing.

The harsh reality is that when the pumpkin in the jug stops growing, it starts to rot. The mother vine, following its divine nature, shifts its life-giving energy to the fruits that are still able to grow.

Sometimes limiting beliefs are transparent and sometimes they are solid as a rock; sometimes they are acquired by accident and sometimes they are adopted by design; sometimes they are modeled and sometimes they are indoctrinated. They often seem true, but on close inspection, they turn out to be just one possibility among many.

I recently suggested to someone who had lost their job that they should start their own business. "Oh, I couldn't do that," was the reply. I pushed the idea. "No, I'm just not cut out for it," they insisted. "My brother-in-law started his own business and he lost everything."

That is called being trapped in your own jug of considerations.

Sometimes life will break your jug for you. An unexpected promotion will demand that you assume responsibilities beyond your comfort level, or a personal tragedy will have you coping with things that you didn't believe you could handle. Suddenly you are out of the jug, growing again.

Yes, there are times and circumstances that favor limiting beliefs, staying jug-bound, but they are chapters in your life, not the whole story. Bigger-than-your-jug opportunities come with risks. If you base your life decisions simply on avoiding risk, you may never leave your jug. There is rot in your future.

Adaptability is wise. Plan to use a belief as long as it serves you, but when it starts to limit growth, reconsider. Maybe what you thought was impossible can actually be achieved. Limiting your own power with inflexible beliefs is unwise.

The value of the Avatar Materials is that they enable you to break your own jug before you begin to rot. How big, how powerful, how successful can you grow? You will never know the answer if you don't break your jug.

# THE STORY OF
# THE AVATAR MATERIALS

*I have enough problems, why worry about spiritual awakening?*

Putting aside all the spiritual reasons, the practical answer is: The closer you come to the state of Source Being*, the more control you have over your life.

When you can experience yourself as distinct from the intellect, you are able to see the patterns of assumptions and beliefs that filter and distort your understanding of (and control over) reality. These assumptions and beliefs, either because they were indoctrinated to serve someone else's interest or because they were embraced in a painful moment of fear and resistance, are rarely beneficial to you. More likely, they are limiting and self-sabotaging. In the worse case, they are completely debilitating. They are hidden from your ordinary awareness, yet collectively, they determine your patterns of behavior and your viewpoint of life.

The first task is discovering the existence of these beliefs (along with the motives that are sustaining them), and the second task is replacing these beliefs with choices made from a self-controlled, discriminating viewpoint. Change your viewpoint, and you can change your life.

*__Source Being:__ an undefinable awareness that creates deliberately.*

*Teaching someone to be flexible in viewpoints, and to reason from different angles, is better than indoctrinating them with a fixed viewpoint. Teaching someone to be flexible in viewpoints involves more work and patience, but in the end you will have a tolerant, compassionate being who reasons well.*

Chapter 8

# Another Way
# Of Looking At Things

The beliefs that you hold, whether deliberately chosen, modeled after another's beliefs, or indoctrinated by authority, create a framework for interpreting and structuring what happens to you, and what you intend for others, and what you find pleasurable or painful. This framework is called a viewpoint or a mind.

**creation:** *the action of defining.*

**discreation:** *a non-action of ceasing to create.*

A viewpoint is a single perspective from which you consider something or someone. It is a particular way of thinking about or approaching a subject.

Consciousness, you will discover, consists of beliefs constructed by multiple viewpoints and each viewpoint possesses some degree of intelligence. Intelligence is the ability to observe, sort, and integrate. Intelligence also is able to predict, and to sustain an intention (motivation). Each viewpoint-plus-intelligence package in consciousness has its own style, unique desires, and, unfortunately, blind spots.

One of the remarkable things that you discover in the Avatar Materials is that there is a natural cascading influence from belief to viewpoint to intelligence. As you improve your ability to manage beliefs, your ability to manage (adopt different) viewpoints improves; and as your ability to manage viewpoints improves, the abilities of your intelligence (problem solving) improve. Beliefs affect viewpoint; viewpoints affect intelligence; intelligence affects your life successes.

Viewpoints determine how you see the world as well as how the world sees you. If you have the belief that "blue people" have wronged you, you are likely to be critical of blue people. Your criticalness will cause people to consider you intolerant. But if you have the belief that "blue people" have helped you, you are likely to praise blue people. Your praise will cause people to consider you kindly.

Unfortunately, how you judge something, or someone, is more often associated with instinctive feelings of righteousness rather than being reasonable. The urge to be right (to occupy one belief) fixes you in a viewpoint and reduces the range of considerations available to your intelligence. When "right" means another is "wrong," you are locking yourself into a viewpoint.

Even if your criticism is on rock-solid ground, it is still likely that it is motivated by something other than observation and reason. A good question to soften asserted rightness and wrongness of a fixed viewpoint is: *Is this something I could be saying about myself?*

Protecting or defending a single viewpoint is a refusal to see something in another way. (This is the beginning of a mind.) When you lock yourself into certain viewpoints, you also lock yourself out of other viewpoints. As you limit your willingness to occupy viewpoints (minds), you also limit your ability to observe, integrate, predict, and intend. Thinking becomes little more than reacting or shuffling old conclusions. Your ability to relate to others is reduced. Your ability to handle life is reduced. Your ability to cope with change is reduced.

How much choice did you have over selecting your current viewpoint? The honest answer is probably, "Not much." A fixed, inflexible viewpoint may work for a short time, but as soon as the circumstances of the world change (as they always do) you become an antique.

Sometimes a little thing, like showing a person how to deliberately change their viewpoint without being struck dumb on the spot, can produce a remarkable recovery of life. Problems disappear and opportunities appear. Adopting another way of looking at something is a simple act that can have magical consequences.

The ability to deliberately change viewpoints is one of the things that the Avatar Materials restores. You can test drive different viewpoints without having to adopt or defend any of them. This is exploring consciousness. You will notice that after testing several viewpoints, there are one or two that you come back to because you find them interesting, or you like the way they feel. These viewpoints that you settle into *after* a broad explo- ration of possibilities are more flexible, confident, and responsible. Trying on different viewpoints civilizes you, and the more you try on, the more tolerant and understanding you become.

*A quick depression cure: repeat "I'm glad I'm not a _____ " five times.*

Do you want to increase your income, your happiness, and your intelligence? Find another way of looking at things.

# THE STORY OF
# THE AVATAR MATERIALS

Avatar.

## How did it start?

In 1987, transcripts of several of my lectures, and
some hastily written research notes, were gathered and
presented as the original Avatar Course. Forgive the
immodesty, but even this early course, as cobbled and
unprofessional as it was compared to our present
curriculum, won instant acclaim from students.

What the course did then, and does even better today,
was set forth instructions for identifying and using certain
mental abilities that everyone more or less possesses.
When these mental abilities are employed in exact
sequences and combinations they literally unlock the
mechanics of experience. Students are able to make (near
instantaneous in some cases) self-determined changes in
their emotional conditions and mental states.

Friends told friends and the news rippled around
the world.

Today (May 1, 2011), The Avatar Course is delivered in
21 languages in more than 72 different countries. Tens
of thousands of people, from all walks of life, have completed the training. A network of 10,000+ Avatar Course
teachers (masters) circles the globe.

*Ranks of angels provide an interesting metaphor for our different thoughts and attitudes.*

Chapter 9

# Thoughts Are Angels

I was thinking about thoughts. Well, actually I was just watching them go by. It occurs to me that there is some hierarchy of thought. Kinds of thought—maybe like the different kinds of clouds. There could be cirrus thoughts, nimbus thoughts, cumulus thoughts or just plain foggy thinking. Totally fogged-in thoughts, zero visibility. Maybe that's the condition of not being able to see beyond our own conclusions.

Anyway, certain thoughts are a lot better—or at least they make you feel better—than other thoughts. The thought, "I was right" feels better than "maybe I was wrong." It's also more effective to think, "I can do it" than it is to think, "I tried and it can't be done."

Some thoughts we create, and some thoughts just seem to come in because someone left the door open. It's as though we each live in a boardinghouse mind, and thoughts are the roomers (play on

words). Some are uninvited guests, and some are more welcome than others. Some of them just stand in the hall and repeat the same line from a song over and over. Do you wonder why you entertain them at all? And when a thought moves in and takes up permanent residence, you have an opinion!

One of the definitions of the word "angel" is a messenger, or thought, from God. In place of thinking of thoughts as intruding guests, we could think of them as angels! We wouldn't be the first to think that way. Instead of saying I had an idea, we could say, "An angel appeared to me." Instead of sharing our thoughts with someone we could share a choir of angels with them. And rather than saying the world began as thought, we could say that the angels built it.

There is a hierarchy of angels that is analogous to the hierarchy of thoughts: ranks of angels corresponding to kinds of thinking.

Let's see if I remember: An archangel is just above an angel, and the next one higher is called a principality—a prince of angels. Then there are "powers," "virtues," and "dominions." And the three top ranks are "thrones," "cherubim" or "cherubs," and "seraphim" or "seraphs."

Cherubim and seraphim are very powerful and guard the throne of the creator. As long as they are on duty, nothing gets by them. Cherubs often are depicted as winged faces, sometimes carrying a flaming sword. Seraphs are described as pure, white-burning love light that cannot be contained.

And whose throne is it that they guard? Who is the ruler of your thoughts? Have you abdicated your throne? What thought sits on your throne? *I am.* And when you rule from your throne, what thoughts protect you and keep you strong? *Love and faith.* They are your cherubim and seraphim!

Angel ranking began in the fifth or sixth century, and most church scholars think it began with a writer calling himself Dionysius the Areopagite. There are many biblical references to angels, particularly in Isaiah, and "winged messengers" are common in hieroglyphs. But it was apparently the Areopagite who cataloged them into nine ranks with each rank responsible for part of creation. I suspect that Dionysius the Areopagite was creating an allegory to avoid offending church elders. Only a select few understood, or even suspected, that there were psychological counterparts to his angel ranks.

I guess we can imagine the kind of thinking that Lucifer, the fallen angel, represents. Have you ever felt that your own thoughts were rebelling against you? Are addictions, desires, and cravings anything other than a descent into the lower regions of self-deceptive thought? Craving thoughts are Lucifer's, right?

I guess if we consider that fallen angels correspond to self-deceptive thinking, we'll get some idea of the direction in which self-deception leads. But before we hit bottom, we can save ourselves by calling forth our cherubim and seraphim (love and faith). These are the mental attitudes that guard our thrones.

So what I was getting at is that there are different kinds of thoughts and different kinds of thinking. You can create a thought. You can just sit there and totally bloom a thought, and it's not necessarily motivated by anything outside of you. It's a thought-angel that you send forth. It's not a thought that is dependent on, or a reflection of, the world around you. It's a thought-angel that you originate.

You can create a thought for no reason (a thought-angel), and then you can create a reason for having created that thought. The second thought is inspired by the first thought (a response), but the first thought—that's your seraph! It was not a response to anything else. It was not a comment or an opinion about reality. It was a thought-angel that you created.

*...there are different kinds of thoughts and different kinds of thinking.*

Now this idea comes as a surprise to some people. They start wondering if their stimulus-response model—where the world is stimulus and thought is response—might have some holes in it. I'd say it does. For one thing, they're going to have a devil of a time explaining where the world that causes them to think "came from." They're going to have to create a creator. That is a pretty neat trick. Let's not go down that path this time. Let's just sit on our I-am-thrones and send our cherubim and seraphim to create the world the way we want it. The world begins as thought-angels. Your thought-angels! That's where reality comes from.

Create the thought, "I am happy." Now that's a seraph thought. You just create it. You don't have to consult reality to see if there is any reason to create it; it is true because you say it is true.

Now create the thought, "I create love." That's a cherub thought. You created it. You also could create, "I can't create love." Either way, the truth of the thought is the thought; it is not dependent on the world.

When you cause you to think, you're God of your universe. You send forth angels.

When the world causes you to think—the world you created—you have fallen into the regions of self-deceptive thought. Do you see the difference? A created thought (an angel) creates a reality, but a response thought creates a lie. What is the lie?

It's simply, "I didn't do it!"

Well, you might be able to pull that on your mother, but you're wasting your time trying to convince me.

When you are God of your universe and you decide something, your angels make it happen. But you have to be God of your universe to do that. Some people try to make something happen with a response thought (a lie) rather than a created thought (an angel). It's the difference between a fantasy and a thought that creates a reality. A thought-angel becomes a fact.

So there is a person on an airplane, and he looks out the window and the engine is on fire. Boy, does that cause some response thinking to occur! "I'm going to crash!" Fortunately, that is only a response thought, if it was his deliberately created thought he wouldn't have a chance. He would have created the fact of the crash.

The way to handle an emergency is to hurry back to your throne and take charge of the angels that have already been created. Something like this:

*Without trying to live by some impossible standard, we simply intend to move in the direction of compassion and sanity. We are not faultless, but we know how to pick ourselves up and keep going.*

"I am. I am on an airplane with an engine on fire. I am frightened. So be it." (Now for some new angels.) "I am going to make it! I am safe! The airplane is safe!"

You have to be a creator to create anything. The question is how powerful of a creator can you become? People who attempt to create "because of..." don't create very much. Mostly they create worries. They worry themselves and they worry others. They will try to convince you that some reality is more powerful than you are. Ultimately, that is a lie.

There is a funny little game that goes on all the time. Someone creates a thought. The thought creates a reality. The reality causes other people to think. Of course, if the reality is getting them to think, they are not the creators of their thoughts. Unless they create that they created the other person to create that reality.

It's a funny little game, don't you agree? You only lose when you won't take responsibility for creating the other guy.

# The Story of
# The Avatar Materials

### How is it different?

The Avatar Materials are more like a passport than a belief system. Their mission is to catalyze the integration of all belief systems.

In the last fifty years a lot of belief systems have been spawned—all sorts of "-isms," "-ologies," and "-ings." Nearly everyone had a favorite and believed beyond a shadow of a doubt that they were on the right path. Well, they were for that moment, but right-path-mentality did very little good for world harmony. Intolerance and separation became a badge of your faith. "You are either with us or you are against us." "You are either part of the solution or part of the problem."

Avatar students quickly comprehend that this black-and-white thinking is headed nowhere. Different stages of consciousness afford different opportunities for growth and development. Belief systems should offer growth experiences, not prison experiences. Avatar is the tool that allows you to fully experience a belief system and then move on.

# Book II:

## Shaping Reality

There are word lessons and there are world lessons. A word lesson is an effort to convey an experience via spoken or written symbols. A word lesson can be informative or enjoyable or inspiring. A word lesson is an expression of someone's belief. A word lesson can be a very nice thing, but it should not be confused with a world lesson.

A world lesson is something that you live through. It's something you encounter and deal with in life, and from the world lesson you emerge changed, more experienced, wiser. A world lesson is an integrated experience. It does not require translation into symbols or sounds for you to remember it. It becomes part of what you know, of how you define yourself to yourself.

Chapter 10

# Elements Of Change

---

I am in favor of facts, but I tend to be leery of
truth. Truth implies *always*, and I really can't see
that far into the future, nor am I clear enough about
everything that has happened in the past to confirm
*always*. So as soon as someone asserts something as
always in all cases true, I begin planning an exit
strategy. "Sorry, I've got to take this call."

Now I'm OK with, and even enjoy, "This is the
way it is for me." That signals that we are dealing
with someone's conviction or personal certainty.
There is probably an interesting story behind the
statement, and listening is easy, because I am not
going to have to confirm, agree, or judge. It is
what it is—another viewpoint.

In the truth department, I am satisfied with: *things
change*. Change happens in the internal world of our
consciousness as well as in the external world of
people, things, and events. This is good or bad
depending upon on your position in regard to it.
If the change threatens or reduces your comfort,
you will probably label it "bad." If the change
brings opportunity, or increases your comfort,
you will probably label it "good." It is a relative
call and subject to... yes, change.

Basically there are two kinds of change, one that you can influence or cause deliberately and one that you can't.

It's not always clear which you are facing. Some things won't budge at first push. A tugboat will churn water for a long time before it influences an oil tanker toward its berth. How hard and long a person is willing to push is a measure of their strength and determination. This differs from person to person, and time to time, and even changes in the same person in response to mental state and circumstance.

## Deliberate Change

From an Avatar viewpoint, the processes governing deliberate change are: labeling, organizing, and controlling—label-it, organize-it, and control-it. Life can be deliberately changed, internally and externally, as long as these three processes are completed successfully.

The label-it process includes naming, shape assigning, and recognizing innate cause-and-effect properties. Naming something is the most obvious function of label-it. Shape assigning is determining the boundaries of the thing (physical or mental) to which the label applies: Some boundaries are suggested by the thing itself, as in the case of an object, and some boundaries are imposed by assignment, e.g. a country's borders. Recognizing the innate cause-and-effect properties includes an assessment of how substantial a thing is, what it will cause, and what effects it can withstand.

The organize-it process includes sorting, aligning, and deciding. The ideal scene one has in mind— goal or purpose—governs organization.

The control-it process includes starting, changing, and stopping efforts, plus the non-effort of ceasing. These three efforts, and one non-effort, govern the reality you experience.

## Discreation (the non-action of ceasing to create)

Because so much of our physical universe survival depends upon resisting, we can become habituated to it. We carry resisting over into our minds and it perpetuates memories and impressions that might better be allowed to wind down, such things as injuries, upsets, losses, and personal vendettas. These stored mental creations influence our actions and decisions for as long as they exist, even if they exist in a stopped state.

Think of the current in a river as a pressure to change. If a boat is to stay in the same place, it must use energy (effort) to resist the pressure of the current. One could say the boat is stopped, but it is still using energy to resist the current.

The steps of discreating mental creations are discovering them, accepting them without judgment, and experiencing them without resistance until the creation ceases to exist. These are the basic mechanics of Avatar's discreate process.

Discreating mental creations (memories, beliefs, identities) will transform your life.

**cease vs. stop**

*cease* to allow something to end or wind down.

*stop* to make something come to an end.

## The Pressure To Change

The pressure to change is variable; it can be slight or it can be substantial, it can be momentary or long lasting. The resistance required to balance the pressure to change also can be slight or it can be substantial, and it can be momentary, or long lasting. These four scales—force of change, duration of change, force of resistance, and duration of resistance—interact to determine the span of time over which a creation will continue to exist. These creations include, but are not limited to, buildings, bodies, emotions, problems, conditions, businesses, and even empires.

For life to survive for any period of time, it must rely on a store of energy, or a continual re-supply of energy, to resist winding down. For something to remain unchanging against the natural pressures of change, it must employ energy to resist the pressure.

Accepting and feeling the flow of change, **as it is happening,** permits you to understand the forces involved and either resist them, redirect them, or flow with them. This is the judo of life. Everything changes, in consciousness as well as the universe. Life and death, creation and destruction, are bold brushstrokes of change. To live forever, or to be dead forever, are equally futile struggles.

If you only resist change, you will eventually experience exhaustion. If you only accept change, you are always a spectator. Living deliberately is shaping change, sometimes accepting, sometimes resisting; the dance of life. You may choose your attitude toward change: Welcome it or resist it, but meet it you must, because everything flows.

To some degree and for some duration, you can deliberately influence reality by increasing or decreasing these four efforts: force of change, duration of change, force of resistance, and duration of resistance. These are skills that you can develop, debug, and enhance with the various Avatar tools.

Chapter 11

# The Mystery School Of Ra

The Avatar Materials are something more than the information and exercises contained in the study packs. Someone could gather all the packs and study them thoroughly. They could look up every word and demonstrate the meaning of every sentence and still they might totally miss the experience of Avatar.

Now isn't that strange?

Let me share a parable. Long before there was anything even resembling culture in the West, there was a highly evolved civilization along the upper Nile in southern Egypt. It was an enlightened civilization governed by teacher-priests. The people were loving, compassionate, and skilled in social fellowship. They looked after each other. How did they achieve this highly evolved state while the rest of the world remained as largely uncivilized barbarians?

The secret was their mystery school of Ra!

*Ra* originally meant "source of consciousness." Only later did it become the hieroglyph for the sun and the name of an Egyptian god. These people reached the pinnacle of civilization, not by technological brilliance, but through their ability to externalize from their reactive impulses and act in alignment with a collective consciousness. They shared experiences that purged them from any desire to do evil. They evolved out of selfish concerns into a broader perspective of life. The teachings and exercises that brought about these changes were contained on a sacred papyrus scroll, which was only studied after the proper initiation by the teacher-priests of Ra.

The word *initiation* means "an initial preparation for instruction." The ritual of an initiation conveys an experience. After you have the experience, words can trigger deeper realizations and clarify the subtilty of the experience. The same words, without the experience, may be meaningless or lead to misinterpretations.

When the initiation ritual is performed correctly, it accomplishes two things. First, it awakens a viewpoint that is more aware than one's habitual viewpoint, and second, it bonds one into a strong fellowship with others who also have been awakened.

The love and safety of the fellowship assists in the removing of the barriers to spiritual evolvement: delusion and prejudice, dishonesty and deception, dishonor and fraud.

So one day, an itinerant trader working the Nile learned about the sacred papyrus scroll. Finding it unguarded, he stole the scroll. Sometime later in his travels, he sold it to a pharaoh-king who ruled in the northern delta region of the Nile. So great was the scroll's rumored powers that the Pharaoh's goldsmiths built a heavy gold chest, encrusted with precious stones, to hold the scroll of plundered wisdom.

Only the most privileged minds of the kingdom were permitted to study the scroll; they argued its meanings, and presented various and contradictory interpretations to the Pharaoh.

The Pharaoh, who was more ambitious for power than knowledge, turned the possession of the scroll into an opportunity. The interpretations became an intellectual foundation, the word lessons, for a new religion that declared Amon-Ra, the sun god, the personal defender of the Pharaoh. A great temple and a ten-meter-tall statue of Amon-Ra were built: A god with the head of a hawk surrounded by the

sun as a crown and bearing, in the crook of its muscular arm, the scepter of the Pharaoh. The people were ordered to sacrifice goats to insure the nation's good fortune. The souls of the goats were ceremonially assigned to Amon-Ra, while the meat quietly found its way into the temple kitchen.

The religion of Amon-Ra was little more than a political tool. Its main body of religious scriptures consisted of explanations of the temple symbols and their meaning: Amon-Ra had the head of a hawk because hawks were known for their keen ability to see; the sun framed Ra because it was the symbol of beginning; the presence of the scepter showed that Amon-Ra and the Pharaoh were allied.

In the name of the new religion, the Pharaoh recruited a powerful army and declared war upon any neighboring tribes who had not accepted Amon-Ra as their chief deity. In reality the Pharaoh was merely levying a tax on the neighboring tribes that he camouflaged as compulsory sacrifices to Amon-Ra. Finally, the Pharaoh, to cement his power, claimed to be the earthly incarnation of Amon-Ra. Temples of Osiris and Aten, older

deities, were either destroyed or re-dedicated to Amon-Ra.

The harsh realities of power, cloaked in the mysteries of the spirit, would rule Egypt for over a thousand years.

And oh, by the way, the sacred scroll was mis-placed, and the gold chest was hammered into a toenail for one of the many statues honoring the nation's Pharaoh-God, Amon-Ra. The precious stones found their way into the purses of wine merchants.

So that is what can happen when people are not properly prepared for spiritual instructions. Without the sincerity that is awakened by honest fellowship and initiation, people interpret new information to support their habitual intentions and ideas. Instead of transforming, they shore up their prejudices with word lessons.

People underestimate the imprisoning ability of the mind. If spiritual awakening were possible within the habitual framework of thinking, all would have it; no external instruction would ever be necessary.

*The spiritual practices of the East have long recognized the difference between intellectual knowledge and real experience. The first they refer to as craving; the latter they refer to as realization.*

# THE STORY OF
# THE AVATAR MATERIALS

### Why does Avatar training stress world lessons over word lessons?

Generally speaking, lessons affect you in some way: You get smarter, or faster, happier, or more skillful. A world lesson impacts you physically with effort and motion, triggers emotional reactions, and then, as you work it through, or think it over later, it affects you intellectually. A world lesson is something that you live through and sort out. You remember it, because it makes sense within the context of your life. You have confidence in it, because it is rooted in your own experience. It becomes an element in your future decisions. It changes attitude and behavior.

A word lesson mainly affects your intellect, and usually ends there. It seldom has any effect physically or emotionally. It does not arise from any experience that you have had. A word lesson is something that someone else sorted out. A word lesson can leave you knowing what the right choices are, but still compulsively making the wrong choices. In the worst case, a word lesson leads to shame and self-loathing rather than self-improvement.

To avoid depression and poor results, self-improvement lessons need to be conveyed experientially rather than intellectually. They need to be understood in the context of your life rather than in the context of a belief system. They need to be taught as skills rather than as revealed secrets. It is unlikely that you will change your life simply by reading or listening.

*What factors are affecting the size of your income,
the passion in your relationships, and the mileage
of your smile?*

## Chapter 12

# Getting Your
# Thinking Straight

*From a 1985 talk by Harry Palmer*

I want to talk to you about something I think
is fantastic. And if you don't believe that it is
fantastic, well, all right, I'm willing to convince
you. We're going to talk about deliberate thinking,
about using the mind as a tool to shape our
experience of physical reality.

Notice, I didn't say perceive reality. I said shape
physical reality. I'm not suggesting you add any
matter or energy to the universe that isn't already
there. What I am saying, and intend to demonstrate to you, is that you can shape what is
already there with your mind.

In order to shape something in the physical
universe, you must first settle on an idea of
the shape in your own mind, walk it through.
You are going to use your mind as a test
simulator. Running and becoming clear on

the simulation is the first step in achieving success, or a lasting relationship, or peace of mind. This is where you get your thinking straight.

I credit my grandfather for the lesson, "First thing, get your thinking straight." He was a respected man and this was his approach to life. He could plow a rocky field with a team of horses or give a Sunday school sermon with equal proficiency. Experience had taught him that you didn't pick up something heavy until you figured out where to put it down. With a little forethought, you could avoid moving something twice if you moved it to the right spot the first time.

*...if your thinking is straight, the chances of making wrong decisions are reduced.*

This is a lesson that my brother and I would have done well to follow. Instead, we struggled to hold up a heavy couch while our mother changed her mind. "Let's try it over here. No. How about over here? No. How about under the window?" Likely as not, we'd end up putting the couch down in the same place we'd picked it up. Then we would both collapse on the couch in exhaustion.

My point is that there are an awful lot of people whose lives are in a collapsed state on that couch. And the reason is because they didn't get their thinking straight first.

Part of straight thinking is making decisions, and everybody knows that is risky. But, if your thinking is straight, the chances of making wrong decisions are reduced. Any reduction in mistakes is welcome.

Most wrong decisions aren't made, they are shuffled into unthinking; then discovered when it's too late to turn around. Wrong decisions lead to failure.

You don't have to make very many wrong decisions before you shut up and follow someone else's directions. Then you can blame them.

For some people, thinking is something that just happens, some spontaneous reaction to something. Their minds are thinking, but there is no direction. Well, you have to have a direction before you can deliberately think something, otherwise you are just bobbing in the currents.

If you give someone a command like, "Think," what do they do? Some people wait for a thought to come along. They haven't quite come up to this idea of deliberately thinking something. Their minds are on autopilot. If you ask them pointedly, "Who is source of your thoughts?" They will tell you something like, "Well, I take a lot after my dad. My mom says I take after my dad." Of course, dad has been dead for ten years. If you are thinking like someone who has been dead for ten years, you are not making much progress.

So you begin working with this guy and you say, "Let's see if you can create a thought. Create a thought about an elephant."

And some mental image of an elephant pops up in his mind from God knows where, probably from a circus or a zoo that he remembers. Notice that he didn't create a new thought about an elephant, he retrieved an old memory about an elephant. You see, for some people this is thinking. You mix memories with perceptions and maybe you recognize something. This is animal-level thinking.

Well, that's okay. Recall is better than just waiting around for another elephant to pass. And being able to select specific memories means that some-one is home in his head. He is awake enough and separate enough to sort through his memories. So you push him just a little harder.

You tell him, "That's good. Now, let's see if you can create something new about that elephant. Put the elephant in swimming trunks, sunglasses, and a baseball cap."

You will instantly see him brighten up. *Whaaat?*

He will be amazed that he can do it. You see, he has been in total agreement with the past and with the universe, and you just pulled him out of the mind, empowered him, and had him create a deliberate thought. Now, if the responsibility of the whole thing does not frighten him too badly, you've got him on the route to Source Being. Soon he will imagine wings for the elephant, turn them neon colors, and have it leading a squadron of butterflies.

So this is how we ease into the concept of deliberate thinking. You don't have to be profound or original; you can be, but you don't have to be. You just have to make sure that it's you who is creating the thoughts. You don't think something "because" or "spontaneously;" you create a thought deliberately that interests you. This is the awakening of creative ability.

It's climbing out of the knock-you-about, cause-and-effect stream of thinking, and realizing that you can be a source. You are the thinker. You can originate a thought that is not a response or reaction to anything that has happened or gone before. And in this moment, you have become the supreme being of your universe. You are the boss.

This is the realization that you have to have to think deliberately: *I am not my mind.* Then if you want to create the thought, "I'm okay," or "I'm happy," you can. Reality will begin to shape itself to your deliberate thinking.

Avatar

Yes, there are some more mechanics to this. If the thought you create is in disagreement with your habitual flow of thinking, you're going to experience some backlash.

Look at it this way. You've placed a thought in the stream of your consciousness, and the currents of the past are hitting it. But as long as you didn't place the thought where the currents are irresistible, and by that I mean you don't try to violate some physical law like gravity, the current of the past can be managed and your thought will shape your experience of future reality.

It all boils down to who is in charge of your consciousnesss. Is it the past? Is it society? Is it the environment? *Or is it you?*

Maybe you will have to apply some effort to shape reality the way you think it. That is okay; at least you know where you are going. You didn't pick up something heavy without any idea of where to put it down. Deliberate thinking, like any ability, improves the more you practice it.

When I tell you to think deliberately, I am not addressing your mind, I am addressing you. The mind is a good tool and storage device, but on its own, it just thinks in circles. So, I don't want to talk to the answering machine, or even your secretary; I want the boss. That's you. It is your mind; you built it, you own it. Now it is time you took control of it.

Who is the supreme being of your universe? You are, of course, but the mind has overthrown you. You have not separated your emotional energy from your thoughts. And now they hop around like a handful of Mexican jumping beans.

Sit still for a minute and try not to think at all. Just decide to sit there for a minute and not think.

Not so easy, huh? Would you buy a computer that you could never turn off? If people drove cars like they run their minds, you might find a Chevy in your bedroom tonight. So your mind is a bit eccentric and doesn't always behave like it ought to. It pretends to be you, gets into worry loops, and entertains ideas, which if they ever saw the light of day would get you locked up.

I understand; I really do understand, and I am going to help you get your thinking straight. For some of you, this is going to mean some minor reality tweaking. For others, this is going to be the beachhead of a major campaign. Are you ready?

Decide that you feel the best you've ever felt. Well?

Do you feel the best you've ever felt? No? It's not so easy, huh?

As soon as you put that idea in your mind—*I feel the best I've ever felt*—your mind reacts with some doubts. You say, "I feel the best I've ever felt," but your mind says, "Wait, that's not true." Who is in charge?

I see some of you are going, "What's this mental stuff got to do with my increasing my income? I want to know how to make more money, and you keep talking about running the mind."

Okay, decide that your income is increasing. What happens?

Your mind says, "Well, we are in a recession and money is scarce and, and, and..."

Who is in charge here, you or the mental machine? Are you shaping reality or are you allowing reality to shape you? Remember, if you can't create a clear idea of something in your own mind, you don't have much of a chance of shaping reality toward that idea. Are you carrying a couch with no place to put it?

In order to control thinking, you are going to have to consciously experience being the thinker. The thinker is you, but it is "YOU" before you defined yourself with thoughts.

*Shape your mind with imagination and faith.*

We are going to call this *big YOU* (Source Being), who is capable to some degree of deliberately thinking. And the little "you's," who are embroiled in thoughts and ideas about themselves and their relationships with the universe, we are going to call *identities*. Identities are dependent on the mind, big YOU is not. Among the identities there is one who protects an idea called "me;" this identity we call the ego.

Ego is almost entirely body-brained-based. That means it is subject to the same influences that affect a body. Things like emotionally indoctrinated desires, resistances, physical perceptions, drugs, electricity, physical damage, frequencies of light and sound, and of course, death. The life of "me" is pretty much a stimulus-response affair. Its principal motivation is selfish, and the only way to change its character is either by pain or pleasure.

Thinking deliberately is the awakening of a non-physical, undefined "I" that exists independent of the mind (Source being).

Source Being, the big YOU, is a powerful creator. It has the ability to step outside the flow of cause-and-effect thoughts and events, and originate new realities. This is new territory. Source Being has the ability to generate an intention that is not the result of any previous cause. Source Being says, "Let there be light." And there is light!

Source Being is obviously a very high state, and to some people it is not real... not yet. Realizing this state has been the goal of contemplative and meditative practices for thousands of years.

Let me show you how to empower a thought in your own mind from source that shapes your experience of reality. Deliberately think, with as much certainty as you can, "I feel the best I've ever felt."

Did you do that? Did some small doubt come to mind following that thought? Yes. Do you have to check with someone or something before you can decide how you feel?

Write the doubt down on a piece of paper exactly as it occurred to you. Don't bother about deciding whether you agree or disagree with the doubt, just acknowledge the fact that there was a doubt and write it down.

If more than one doubt shows up, write them all down, and acknowledge each one.

Now, deliberately think again, "I feel the best I've ever felt." Think it with as much certainty as you can. "I feel the best I've ever felt." Write down any doubts that occur to you and acknowledge them.

*Questioner: How do I acknowledge them?*

**Harry:** Just write OK after each one of them. Write OK like you are the president and you are signing off on some request that you are granting. Scribble OK and initial it. Remember, you are the boss.

All right, again, deliberately think, "I feel the best I've ever felt." Think it with as much certainty as you can. If there are still doubts, write them down and acknowledge them.

Repeat this as long as you have doubts. Not feeling that the statement is true is a doubt.

*Questioner: I'm having some trouble because I have this pain in my back, and it's hard to feel the best I've ever felt with that pain there.*

**Harry:** Write that down just the way you told me, "I'm having some trouble because I have this pain in my back, and it's hard to feel the best I've ever felt with that pain there."

After you've written it down, scribble your presidential OK and once again deliberately think, with as much certainty as you can, "I feel the best I've ever felt."

*Questioner: It's hard to get much certainty because of the pain.*

**Harry:** That's fine. Write down, "It's hard to get much certainty because of the pain." And scribble your OK as the boss. Now, deliberately think again, "I feel the best I've ever felt."

(Pause) What's happening?

*Questioner: Well, it's getting better, but I still think about the pain.*

**Harry:** Write down, "It's getting better, but I still think about the pain." And sign off on it.

*Questioner: No matter what I say, you are going to tell me to write it down.*

**Harry:** That's right. As long as there is some non-deliberate thinking arising in your mind, I'm going to ask you to write it down and sign off on it. You know why? Because I know you are the boss, and you can create anything you choose. Would you like to feel the best you've ever felt?

*Questioner: I don't know.*

**Harry:** What are your considerations on it?

*Questioner: There have been times when I've felt awfully good.*

**Harry:** Yes.

*Questioner: If I could only feel that way once, I wouldn't want to waste it.*

**Harry:** Yes.

*Questioner: I really don't think I could feel that good with the pain in my back.*

**Harry:** Yes. Now, once again, with as much certainty as you can, deliberately think: "I feel the best I've ever felt."

(Pause) Did you do it?

*Questioner: (laughing) This really is fantastic.*

**Harry:** Yes, I told you that.

*Questioner: Well, even though I'm skeptical and have been saying how I couldn't, or didn't want to, I realize that I do feel the best I've ever felt.*

**Harry:** Are you sure?

*Questioner: Yeah, even the back pain is gone. It just disappeared. How did you do that?*

**Harry:** You did it. I just coached you to do it.

**Harry:** *(addressing a lady in the front row)* How do you feel?

*Lady: I feel good.*

**Harry:** Do you feel the best you've ever felt?

*Lady: I was afraid of what I might do if I felt that good.*

**Harry:** That is a wonderful doubt. I'll write it down for you, "I was afraid of what I might do if I felt that good." Are you ready to sign off on that one?

*Lady: Yes! I feel the best I've ever felt. I really do.*

**Harry:** Yes, you do.

If there is anyone here who doesn't feel the best he or she has ever felt, keep writing and signing off. I'm sure you're only a few doubts away from success.

From your smiles, I can tell that most of you are feeling the best you've ever felt, so this is a good place to end. Thank you very much.

# THE STORY OF
# THE AVATAR MATERIALS

### Why should I consider doing The Avatar Course?

Avatar is a powerful and extremely effective course that is based on the simple truth that your beliefs will cause you to create or attract the situations and events that you experience as your life.

The goal of the course is to guide you in an exploration of your own belief systems, and to equip you with the tools to modify those things that you wish to change. The Avatar Course opens a window on the inner workings of your own consciousness. The abilities and skills you develop on the course will help you re-structure your life.

The Course teaches world lessons (experiential) rather than word lessons (intellectual). For this reason it requires a trained Avatar Master to guide you into the actual lessons that are already contained in your own consciousness.

Chapter 13

# Connected By Time

Psyche scarring from horrible events can leave you with fixed considerations that interfere with your evaluation of present time events. Because a classmate with black hair rejected you, and spread lies about you in school, do you now expect the worst from people with black hair? Because a dog bit you when you were little, do you now live a life that is occasionally deflected by an involuntary fear of dogs?

How do you remove the influences of the past on your present-time consciousness? Is it possible to re-evaluate the considerations that arise from your memories? Experienced explorers of consciousness agree, "Yes you can!"

The injuries and humiliations that you suffered in the past are over and gone. Time and circumstance have changed and so can you. Here is one of those "secrets of the ages" that Avatar students keep discovering: *How much you let the past affect you is under your control.*

"Now wait a minute, Harry," you say. "Some of the things that happened to me were horrible events."

*True.*

"No one should have to experience them."

*True.*

"The reason I still consider them (consciously or unconsciously) in my evaluation of current events is to keep the horrible event from happening again."

*Not always true. In fact your fixed considerations actually set you up with expectations of the horrible event reoccurring. Expectations can shape how you experience reality.*

Let me tell you a story. As a kid, my parents were encouraged by the local medico to pay him to surgically remove my appendix. I guess his operation statistics were down, or he needed the cash, or maybe the practice. A little speech on the dire consequences of an erupted appendix was given to my parents and they caved and dutifully signed a release on my behalf. A few hours later I was admitted to the hospital for an appendectomy.

The backwater country hospital still used diethyl ether as an anesthetic, dripping it on gauze held over your nose. Now I was only four, but I was a fighting four. The prospect of being gassed in an operating room was not something I was about to submit to peaceably. Unfortunately, there were more of them than there were of me. I was soon gagging and swirling off into a vortex of blackness. Dying would have been no more unpleasant.

Roughly the same scenario played out two years later with a tonsillectomy. I was semi-cajoled into that by the promise that I could have all the strawberry ice cream that I could eat following the procedure. You know the deal with that, you can't swallow after a tonsillectomy.

So I came out of these two traumas with the firm conviction that ether was the worst smelling, most noxious chemical that anyone could ever inhale. Once when a teacher opened a bottle of ether in the chemistry lab, I had to leave. And I couldn't even walk by a hospital. A whiff of ether and I started puking.

My truth about the smell of ether was that it was awful, but to my surprise, the dictionary defined it as, "...a pleasant smelling, colorless, volatile liquid." Pleasant smelling! You are kidding me. Maybe someone would describe a goat as pleasant smelling, but ether?

Then in college I met a redheaded co-ed that was studying pre-med and she invited me to a party. "It will be very cool," she said. "It is being held by a group of med students that are very avant-garde." Hey, who is going to turn down a good-looking redhead? Well?

The surprise came when we arrived at the party and I discovered that these avant-garde medicos were mellowing the party by evaporating ether into the room. The redhead was delighted. Can you believe that? Me? I gagged, stumbled out the door, and puked in the stairway. An inglorious exit and an abrupt end to what might have been an adventurous relationship. My past considerations had nailed me.

Several years later, I had the opportunity to relive the childhood operations that were performed

*Respect dissolves resistance.*

under ether. After releasing my resistance to the "horrible events," I was able to change my consideration about the odor of diethyl ether. It became a neutral event with me. Experiencing my own resistance allowed me to re-evaluate the consideration that I was carrying from the past.

So again I ask, are psychic scars real? Yes, as long as you don't remove them by an effective re-evaluation technique. The elements of the past that affect our mental outlooks are the ones that we resist experiencing and thus carry forward in time.

Avatar Wizard Course students, Orlando, FL, January 2010

# THE STORY OF
# THE AVATAR MATERIALS

### What is a belief?

A belief has definition and influence; it is the building block of consciousness. Believing is the action of structuring a mind.

Beliefs have the capacity to stimulate impressions, or to filter impressions, or to react to other creations. Beliefs that have the capacity to stimulate or react to other creations are called viewpoints.

A habitual viewpoint is called a self. The identity, or personality, of the self is formed by the beliefs. The more defined and inflexible the beliefs, the more defined and inflexible the identity. The more flexible the beliefs, the more flexible the identity.

Behind viewpoint is the timeless, space-less, mass-less, energy less awareness that underlies all creation. It perceives by becoming the thing perceived. In this mode of perception there is no separation between the perceiver and the perception. Perception is the same as being.

Realities are projected from viewpoints. Viewpoints react and interact with their own projected realities to produce the phenomena of energy, space, and time.

Chapter 14

# A Talk On Sensory Deprivation And Mental Bodies

First, for those of you who are not familiar with sensory deprivation tanking, it's an eight-foot-long sealable tank with about ten inches of very high-density salt water. You float on your back in the salt water. The air and the water are adjusted to about 94 degrees, which is the same temperature as your skin.

If you put your hand in a pan of 94-degree water, you can't tell if it's hot or cold.

The tank is sound proof, at least as far as external sounds. If you concentrate, you can hear the sound of your own heart. The tank is completely black. In this absence of light it's difficult to determine if your eyes are opened or closed.

When you float in the tank, the sensory inputs that you normally get from the eyes, ears, and skin disappear—the senses are deprived of physical stimulation.

So after two hours in the tank I thought, "So what's the big deal? Here I am floating in this dark tank."

I still feel my body floating here... or can I?

It slowly occurred to me that my attention had shifted from feeling my physical body to feeling the idea that I had of my physical body. I could feel my "thought of a body" as if it were a body.

**Audience:** Could you say that again?

It is confusing at first. Let me explain this way. I have a physical body that gives me sensory feedback. If I touch something hot, the skin sends a signal to my brain and I pull my hand away. My body's senses are responding to physical universe stimuli.

Now the idea of the tank was to interrupt the connection between the body's senses and the physical universe. There were no physical universe stimuli, yet I was feeling parts of my body.

The tank was working, but I still had a mental idea of the body, and it was giving me simulated feedback that I mistook for feedback from a physical body—a mental form of virtual reality. Of course, since there was no physical stimulation, it was all happening in the mind.

I found this discovery that I had a "mental copy body" of my physical body very interesting. And when the actual, physical sensory feedback was eliminated by the sensory deprivation experience, the mental concept of a body just slid in so subtly that at first I didn't notice it.

**Audience:** Wow.

Yeah, wow. That's what I was thinking. *Wow!* Two superimposed body forms, one mental and one physical. I think we all have them.

When they give identical feedback, there's no problem. You just consider all the feedback is coming from the sensory organs of the physical body. The mental body backup is just duplicating the physical body or vice versa.

But what happens when the physical body and backup are not identical? What happens when your mental body gives you different feedback than your physical body?

If your brain receives the signal *my foot hurts,* you assume this is coming from your physical body, but what if it's not? What if you examine your foot and can't find anything wrong with it, but it still hurts? What if the pain you are experiencing is coming from your mental body? Maybe the mental body is storing an old picture of a foot injury that is still sending pain signals to your brain.

Remember the commercial for recording tape? *Is it real or is it Memorex?* Your brain can't always tell.

Is the sore foot you are experiencing coming from something wrong with your physical body, or is it an old picture of a foot injury being remembered and transmitted from the mental body? Do you see where this is going?

Does this clarify the phenomenon of phantom-limb pain? Does this clarify the source of psychosomatic aches and pains? Are they coming from painful memories in the mental body that are being confused with the physical body? I think so.

**Audience:** So if something hurts and there is no physical reason for it, it is probably coming from the mental body?

That's what I am thinking. The two sources, mental and physical, can be confused. Imagined pain created from traumatic memories and real physical pain look pretty much the same to a brain. Can you see that if the brain didn't know whether the sensation was coming from the foot or your imagination, it might be confused?

The mental body is a mixed construction of painful memories and imagination. It contains trauma and consideration about past experiences. When these mix or override your present-time sensory feedback, you get strange conditions that don't respond well to treatment.

My guess is that this can be made to work both ways. Mental considerations could either delay healing or speed it up. Deliberately created considerations in a mental body like, *this foot is healthy and strong*, could speed healing, just as a consideration from a traumatic memory like, *my foot hurts*, might delay healing.

**Audience:** Can you give us another example of a traumatic memory consideration?

Sure. The physical body breaks a leg on a rock. The mental body stores a picture of the incident and creates the consideration that you have to be careful around rocks.

Most, if not all, of the considerations stored in the mental body are reminders to avoid certain circumstances that in the past proved injurious to the physical body.

If you had this must-be-careful consideration and went rock climbing, just the slightest touch of a rock to the leg could set your leg to aching. But, you see, it's not the touch of the rock to your physical leg that is giving you the feedback of pain, it's the feedback you're getting from your mental body.

The consideration in the mental body causes you to say, "My leg hurts." And guess what happens if you say that enough times? It becomes true. The physical structure of your body actually begins to transform into some condition that justifies the origination, "My leg hurts."

**Audience:** How would you handle that?

One way would be to raise a person's awareness sufficiently, that they could differentiate between the feedback they are getting from the physical body and the feedback they are getting from the mental body. That's the goal that we are working toward when we familiarize ourselves with the operation of our own minds.

Another handle is you could just stay in present time. The more present you are with what is happening, the less chance of any hidden memories having an influence on your sensory feedback.

*secondary: a reaction to a deliberately created thought*

Once you are trained in the Avatar Materials you can just say as source, "My leg is fine." Then when the consideration, "My leg hurts," shows up as a secondary, you discreate it. Using the tools you recognize and acknowledge the contradictory consideration, and slide it right back into the past where it belongs. "My leg did hurt, but now it's fine."

# THE STORY OF
# THE AVATAR MATERIALS

### Where did the title "ReSurfacing" come from?

If you've ever done any scuba diving, you probably know the exhilaration that occurs when you finish the dive and begin your slow ascent. A number of things happen during the ascent. There is a natural relaxation as the pressures reduce, the light grows brighter, the sound of your breathing has a quieting effect on the mind. From below, the surface of the water is the limit of one reality. Resurfacing is at once a crossing over, a leaving, and a returning.

I chose the title because of those feelings. I think the ocean, with its currents, secrets, and depths, is also a good analogy for consciousness. The ReSurfacing processes are a path of ascent through the levels and currents of oceanic consciousness back into pure awareness.

*In the first decade of Avatar, 1986 to 1996, there were six Wizard courses held in Orlando, Florida. These were profound experiences that changed the lives of the individuals that attended, as well as magically influencing circumstances and events beyond the walls of the hotel.*

*One feature of the Wizard experience was the morning talks. The following is excerpted from a talk on power that Harry gave on January 27, 1995.*

Chapter 15

# Preserving Your Creative Source Power

All beings begin each life with some allotment of creative power. Most of us, through unawareness, ignorance, or worse, waste this power in pointless contests, or in building metaphoric sandcastles that disappear in the next tide. Our minds are clouded with indoctrinated beliefs and persistent identities that keep us in conflict and turmoil. Bullets and fate claim their shares.

Living deliberately requires courage, wisdom, and ambition. At the core of courage is the ability to perceive what is, as it is, while staying present and aware. You do not run away and hide. At the core of wisdom is the ability to predict the long-term consequences of actions, and the human reactions they will cause. At the core of ambition is vigorous, focused effort. Increase these qualities, keep them in balance, and you will recover your power to create and shape realities.

These three qualities need to be balanced. Ambition alone will always destroy itself. Look at the direction of this planet if you doubt me. Wisdom without courage grows out of date. And courage without wisdom never sees the bigger picture. When these qualities are kept in balance, they result in a power that will accelerate your evolvement, rather than your destruction.

Yes, we all know that power can be dangerous. It can be corrupted and misdirected. So before you throw your Wizard lightening bolts, I want to give you some advice on how to manage and preserve the power that you are recovering from your processing. How do you keep it from flashing back? How do you employ it to prevent digging yourself an even deeper hole?

I'm going to suggest four personal qualities that you can develop to preserve the creative source power of a mind. If you sincerely practice these qualities they will reveal priceless secrets.

## The first quality is simplicity.

The Taoist symbol for simplicity is an uncarved rock; it is potential that does not carry any fixed definition. Shedding definition is letting go, not defending any idea of your self, and not investing

in a fixed viewpoint. When your mind is not forced
into expressions of judgment or pretense, it will
quiet and flow with what is present. Compulsive
desires will disappear. Letting go of justifications
and arguments will bring your mind back to the
present. Ask simple questions. Give simple
answers. Share simple pleasures. Enjoy the things
that money can't buy. Observe. Be an uncarved
rock (minus the rock).

## The second quality is integrity.

Know such wholeness that nothing is favored
because of hidden mental influences. Bring
your mind into the light. Stop being your story.
Recognize your connection to everyone and everything. Make dishonesty and denial of responsibility
unthinkable. Stay present. Be outside of time
rather than in it. Don't create effects that others
are unwilling to experience. Use gradients. Turn
your criticisms around and own them; the faults
you find in others are your keys to understanding
the mind with which you are associating.

## The third quality is service.

Release your mind from the slavery imposed
by the ego. You are not matter, energy, or space.
You are beyond any definition, so why be a slave
to one? Allow yourself the gift of universal perspective. Wisdom will appear and your actions will be
motivated by an intuitive, spontaneous, benevolent
intent. There is no regret. Do useful things. Help
others for the delight of helping others. Concentrate
on adding value to the world rather than consum-
ing the world.

## The fourth quality is acceptance.

Certain things in life are unavoidable: mistakes, losses, injuries, injustices, emotional upsets, horrors, pains, overwhelms, and of course, death. Resisting what is unavoidable only causes it to last longer and leave deeper scars. But how do you accept suffering? The answer is that you must find something positive about it. At first, this may seem impossible, but, if you approach the experience with courage and use your Avatar tools, it is possible.

Finding the positive in a resisted experience may require that you forgive someone, or confess a transgression, or assume a broader perspective. Transforming a negative experience into something positive causes you to grow.

SIMPLICITY
INTEGRITY
SERVICE
ACCEPTANCE

# THE STORY OF
# THE AVATAR MATERIALS

### What are "primaries" and "secondaries"?

A primary is an origination that is issued with sufficient intention that it creates a reality for the originator. It is a tool for shaping experiences. For example, "I am happy," and the originator becomes happy.

A secondary is something that is created other than what is intended. It is an obstacle that is stirred up by a primary. The feeling of disappointment is a secondary. For example, "I am happy," and the originator feels disappointed that he didn't become happy.

Secondaries can be processed until they no longer arise, and the primary creates.

# THE STORY OF
# THE AVATAR MATERIALS

**What is a "source primary"?**

*I am source* is a redeeming primary.

The redeemed is the one, who while waiting for redemption, discovers that he or she is the redeemer. This may sound blasphemous to anyone who cannot fathom that they are the determiner of their life circumstances.

Redemption is the delivery of a being from the belief *I am effect* (and all the beliefs that support this belief) to *I am source*. When this source primary creates, really creates, one will experience the deepest level of being.

*The Avatar Course is nothing more or less than an escape from a mind trap, which you have been caught in for so long that you have forgotten what freedom feels like.*

Chapter 16

# Belief and Experience

The connection between belief and experience is not always obvious. Most peoples minds' are bombarded from an early age by what they should believe. Many of these suggestions are dutifully recorded by the mind and re-broadcast as beliefs as circumstances warrant.

Believing is such a powerful creation process that even agreeing with what someone else suggested seems to attract that experience into your life. Once that happens, the belief wheel begins: What you believe attracts an experience that strengthens your conviction that what you believe is true. The indoctrination trap is complete. Good night, Source Being. The flow of creation is flowing in on YOU.

Wouldn't it be nice if everyone realized that what he or she believed had a direct consequence on the reality he or she was experiencing? People have difficulty with this idea because it is a higher-level realization that rests on earlier realizations.

One of the earlier realizations is that YOU and your body are not the same. The brain is an organ in your body; it is not YOU. The body is a biological marvel, a product of evolution and genetics. It converts matter into energy via the process of digestion and uses that energy to power the various systems in the body, including the body's sensory arrays and its immune system. The human body is truly an incredible organism, but... it is not YOU.

The more familiar you become with the body, the more clearly you will realize that it is not YOU. This is the missing realization in some people's lives.

The second earlier realization is that YOU and your mind are not the same. This separation is easily missed because YOU and your mind trade off on running your life—at least they did until the mind took over. Once the mind is in charge, it is a dictator who does not relinquish power without a battle.

Mind is a databank of knowledge and memories, and in its usurper role as emperor of your life, it generates thoughts and emotions based on its knowledge and memories. Mind appears to originate thoughts and ideas, but it is more of a re-mix and re-broadcast of habitual behaviors than new creations. Most of the mind's content comes from experience, but not all. Some can come directly from YOU.

So YOU are not the body, not the mind; YOU are the boss, a Source Being, the think-*er*, the believe-*er*, the realize-*er*. Source Being is an awareness with abilities but without definition. You are YOU, and YOU are awesome! It is a secret worth discovering.

One of the most powerful "-*er*" abilities YOU have is identify-*er*. You have the power to become whatever you put your attention on. Placing this power on automatic is how YOU fell into the mind trap and became a story. YOU surrendered your creative power and began believing what you were told to believe. YOU went from creator to creation. YOU became dependent upon the external universe for your beliefs.

Like the body, the more familiar YOU become with your mind, the more clearly you will realize that it is a substitute (a stand in) for YOU, but not the real YOU.

Waking up YOU clarifies the connection between belief and experience. YOU don't have to shape your beliefs according to experience; on the contrary, YOU can shape experience according to your beliefs.

The mind's creative power is based upon conviction from experience; your creative power is based upon certainty, faith. YOU are a creator, a Source Being, and YOU do not have to consult or confer with any existing reality to create a new belief in your own mind. YOU can make a primary.

The mind (heavily burdened with experience) asks, "What should I believe?" YOU ask, "What do I want to experience?"

You plant a belief-primary of what you want to experience in your own mind. Your mind may object with a few secondaries, but if you handle the secondaries properly, your originated belief will take root and the mind will begin to create, or attract, the experience that will verify its new belief.

As YOU learn to manage your mind's beliefs, more and more of the elements of life will come under your control. States of being, identities,

**primary:** *an origination that is issued with sufficient intention that it creates a reality for the originator.*

**secondary:** *something that is created other than what is intended. It is an obstacle that is stirred up by a primary.*

attitudes, behaviors, perceptions, physiology, relationships, and even other people, can be shaped by the primaries you make. You can create your mind into a reality-shaping tool by planting empowering beliefs. Yes, you can.

Sorting out all of the above can be a daunting task. You will find that the Avatar tools will be of great assistance. Once the mind is sorted out (and it should be sorted out) you will find yourself with a new dilemma. What do I want to create?

| To influence: | Suggested Primary: |
|---|---|
| States of Being | I am source. |
| Identity | I am happy to be me. |
| Attitude | My actions are naturally right. |
| Behaviors | I am helpful to others. |
| Perception | I see and think clearly. |
| Physiology | My body is healthy. |
| Relationships | I like people and keep my word. |
| Other people | My life benefits others. |

Chapter 17

# Primaries and Domains

*From a 1997 Wizard lecture*

A domain is a sphere or area of activity. It's an area for which you assume some responsibility and in which you have some influence. There are physical domains and consciousness domains. We are going to start by talking about physical domains.

Similar domains, by definition, are in the same range of magnitude, such as farms in a valley. Each farm is the domain of one farmer who works the farm and makes the decisions about plantings and harvests. The farmer assumes some responsibility for the farm and has some influence on what is grown or produced.

The farmer may have employees who work in his domain, but they have lesser amounts of influence. You could create a scale of the influence each participant has in a particular domain. For instance, the farmer is the boss and makes the major decisions, the farm foreman gives orders to the workers, and the workers do what they are told. We are describing three levels of participation in this domain. The

farmer, the foreman, and the workers are all operating in the same domain, but they each have different powers of influence over the events in that domain.

You could change domains. Say the foreman has his own farm, and the first farmer goes to help with the foreman's harvest. The farmer, moving from the domain of his farm to the domain of the foreman's farm, changes his role. He goes from being the boss to being the worker.

The two farms are domains in the same range of magnitude. We could call them family farms.

What would happen if the first farmer went to help the foreman and, forgetting what domain he was in, tried to participate as the boss? Uh-oh, friction. Maybe an argument. How would you feel if your neighbor came into your house and told you what TV channel you had to watch? Maybe you would say, "Not in my domain, you don't."

The participants in a domain work out their own right-to-influence scale. It may be arrived at by competition, as it is in nature, or it may be arrived at by agreement, as it is, ideally, among friends. There are also chance ways of establishing right-to-influence scales such as the flip of a coin.

You could call any of these right-to-influence scales the politics of the domain. Anytime you have a domain with more than one participant, you are going to have politics.

There are also domains of different magnitude.

Domains in the same order of magnitude often form collectives. The collective, taken as a whole, is a domain of greater magnitude. The president of the farmer's cooperative operates in a domain of greater magnitude than that of the farmer.

*A primary is the appearance of a creation.*

So we've got two ideas here. We have the idea of *influential power within a domain,* and we have the idea of *different magnitudes of domains.*

*A secondary is the reappearance of a creation.*

In the domain of the bow and arrow, the best archer had the most influence. However, when he stumbled into the domain of the cannon, he quickly lost his influence. The cannon is a different magnitude of domain.

Another example of a domain in a different order of magnitude is the county or the province in which our farms exist. The reason we call a county or province a different order of magnitude is not just because of its size—you could have a farm the size of a county. The real difference is in the magnitude of influence. A county commissioner has a greater magnitude of power to influence events than a farmer has.

The next higher level of domain might be the state in which the county is located. Again, this is a change in order of magnitude. The state governor has greater magnitude of influence than a county commissioner has.

You not only have a pecking order within a domain, but you actually have a pecking order of magnitudes of domains.

Even though the governor is the political boss in the domain of the state, and the farmer is the political boss in the domain of the farm, they have different magnitudes of influence.

The president of the country has more power to influence than the governor of the state has, because the country is a domain of greater magnitude than the state.

If the farmer looks across the valley and makes the primary, "I'm going to build a hydroelectric dam," what's going to happen? The other farmers are going to object. His neighbors are going to turn into secondaries. He doesn't really have the power to create that primary, because it's outside his domain. He's going to have to work very hard to handle his neighbors' secondaries.

The governor can look across the same valley and make the primary, "I'm going to build a hydroelectric dam." Some farmers may object to having their land flooded, but he is the governor and their objections are just very small secondaries. He restates his primary a few times, pays the farmers off or throws them in jail—he doesn't need their agreement—and starts construction on the dam. If you're governor, you're not going to let a few protesting farmers spoil your dam primary.

Unfortunately, the valley the governor picked to build a dam is one of the favorite vacation spots of the president. Suddenly the governor finds an executive order on his desk halting construction on the dam. This dam secondary is coming from the president who operates in a greater domain.

Have you ever tried to make a primary and run into secondaries from a domain that is a magnitude above the domain you are operating in?

Have you ever had an Avatar student complain because his primary to win the lottery didn't work? You see, he's on the farm, and he's trying to run the country.

I once had a student ask me if I could levitate. I had to say no. What I should have said was, "Do you have the power to declare war on Canada?"

If you make the primary, "When I drop my pencil it will fall to the ceiling," what's going to happen? A secondary called gravity.

It's not a matter of faith that your pencil doesn't fall upward. It's a violation of the rules of a greater domain than the one in which you are operating. Again, you're trying to issue a presidential order from the domain of the farmer. It's like saying to the hired man, "Plant the oats, feed the chickens, and then balance the national budget." Different domains!

I think it would be safe, at least for now, to say that every domain defines a sphere in which you have the freedom to create, but also defines the limits of your creating. Learning the freedoms and limits of the domain you are operating in is called living.

When you repeatedly come up against the limits of the domain you are operating in—meaning your primaries are overwhelmed by secondaries from a more powerful domain—it is time to move up an order of magnitude. Time to play a bigger game.

# Book III:

## Marketing Enlightenment

If you experience yourself as a creator, you will transcend the world. If you create yourself as an experiencer, you will become a definition in the world. Those are the two extremes of a very popular game called living.

Both are processes that can be divided up into a number of steps.

*When we first started to deliver Avatar to the public, we considered that it was a good product, that it had many years of research behind it, and that it was simple to apply. The processes and exercises were amazingly effective at changing conditions. The course was self-paced, and respectful of what people already knew or believed. Those qualities made the course integrative rather than confrontational. People loved doing the course, and they told their friends about it. That was the beginning.*

Chapter 18

# The Evolution Of The Avatar Course

*Opening address to The Professional Course by Harry Palmer*

What I would like to talk to you about is the evolution of Avatar and my own personal evolution. There seems to be some connection.

In 1986, the trainers and I had just come out of a ten-year stint of poverty working 60 and 70 hour weeks for a religious organization, which for one reason and another, I had lost faith in. That's another whole story, but the point is I was tired of manipulative religions, hypocritical ministers, and non-profit organizations, especially the non-profit part.

Actually, I had drifted away from that organization several years before the other trainers, and I was quietly waiting for them to either confirm my skepticism or to renew my faith. Well, you know how that went. During that fence-sitting period, I began exploring the world as a small-business entrepreneur. In three years I started five businesses, all of which were more or less successful, but not very exciting.

So that is where I was in 1986. I was pretending to be a member of a religion that I didn't believe in; I was running businesses that I didn't enjoy; and I was waking up every morning feeling that the answers to life were slipping a little further away. Some of you have been there. That's the dark cloud part.

The silver lining was that this state of affairs led me back to my study of eastern philosophy and into sensory deprivation research, all of which eventually came together in the creation of The Avatar Course. I've pretty well covered this period in the book "Living Deliberately."

Let me describe the motivation behind our early delivery of The Avatar Course. We had a breakthrough mind training course that we could teach people to use, and they would pay us for the instruction and experience. The course was so effective that we offered a money-back guarantee. And there were virtually no takers. Graduates raved about the results, and with little or no advertising we continued to grow rapidly.

We had a simple business plan: People would pay us tuition, and we would ensure that they understood the materials and knew how to use them. It was a win-win transaction. Our marketing plan was that satisfied students would tell others, and those others would want to do the course. It worked and was unstoppable.

Now you will have to excuse my immodesty, but the reason why this worked so well was because no one else in the world was offering a mind training program that even came close to being as straightforward, simple, and effective as The Avatar Course. So we grew confident and probably even a little arrogant... okay, maybe a lot arrogant.

I imagined that our customers would say, "Harry, I see that I was mentally blocking myself, and now I realize I can create the life I desire."

And I'd say, "Thank you very much for taking the course. We're glad you enjoyed it." And the deal was done. But we had underestimated the benefits that delivering Avatar had on our own lives. We got better at instructing and the product continued to evolve until it worked better than we had imagined.

One day a prominent New York psychiatrist, who had sent his entire staff to do The Avatar Course, pulled me aside and with the most excitement I ever saw him display, exclaimed, "Do you really know what you've got here? Do you have any idea of what you have discovered? You're teaching methods of consciousness transformation that are more effective than anything I learned in eight years of training in psychotherapy."

So maybe now you understand why we were arrogant.

Days or weeks after finishing the course, people's understanding of what they had experienced continued to grow. They realized they were truly free from their old restraints. Some experienced an ego-free consciousness. I paid attention. Their energy levels shot up. We received the sweetest letters describing how they had used the tools to create miracles in their own lives and in other people's lives.

At first, we considered the letters were just good marketing endorsements, but they were more than that. They were insights from people who were learning to turn the struggles and suffering of their lives into valuable lessons. And they wanted to share their transformation. That's how The Avatar Master Course came about.

Avatars were not only experiencing themselves as the source of their own thoughts and beliefs, they were edging up on the mystical experience of a cosmic source. After several hours of running one of the processes, one student commented, "I feel like I'm in god territory."

The majority of Avatar graduates continued to evolve into higher, wiser, more peaceful people. They gained confidence in their abilities to create. They felt secure, some for the first time in their lives. They made decisions without encountering guilt or doubts. They learned to align beliefs and actions with a goal. They became appreciative of life, and many became financially successful. They were awake and ready to participate in creation.

Sometimes when the graduates shook my hand, they were reluctant to let go. They would look into my eyes with a fully awake look that asked, "What should I do now? Is there something in the world that needs to be done?"

And I turned myself inside out looking for the answer to that question. Is every attempt to better the world really just a resistance to be discreated? Is it enough to return to the peace and calm of one's own center and just watch the world proceed? Appreciating all, understanding all, forgiving all, beyond it all? Or is there something more to be done?

That is the question behind the look. That is what kept people holding my hand and wondering into my eyes. *What do we do now? We have found the answers we were seeking, what do we do with them? In the past, we kept ourselves asleep by not knowing, but now we know.*

I think that when you pose a question with enough sincerity, and are willing to have it answered, the universe will find a way to answer you. Was there something more that I would like to do?

An answer came back to me. It came in a dream image of a holy man who spoke to me in an Indian accent. He said, "The collective consciousness is not in your head. Your head is in the collective consciousness."

After I had repeated that a few times, I began to understand. It is not enough to work on self. There is a point where personal evolvement must go beyond self-examination into social responsibility. The collective consciousness is not in your head. Your head is in the collective consciousness.

The long handshakes and the looks from the Avatar graduates drifted back to me and began to make sense. They are evolving beyond self-examination. They have made it through the labyrinth of self-delusions. They are awake in the present and looking at the world.

So in its own way the universe explained why the Avatar graduates were sticking around. The question came down to this: If you have somehow acquired the ability to create a civilization that is more peaceful, wise, and of higher quality than what exists, is it responsible to go sit on a beach and contemplate your navel?

So today when the Avatar graduates give me that questioning look, I look right back and say, "I'm contributing to the creation of an enlightened planetary civilization. Would you like to join me?" Wow, would they ever!

This awakening to broader responsibility is why our Avatar Master courses are full. People get stars in their eyes when they think about delivering Avatar. It is fantastic. How would you like to present someone you care about with the experience that, knowingly or unknowingly, they have been seeking for lifetimes? Oh, and get paid for doing it.

Delivering Avatar as a for-profit business is a good thing all around. You are contributing to something worthwhile, but you're not doing it as an unappreciated sacrifice. I think that's why the Avatar Network keeps growing. It delivers a paid-for training that is free of hidden obligations, belief systems, or guilt trips.

*To create an enlightened planetary civilization, we must overcome primitive urges that once were crucial to the evolutionary path, but are now impediments—anxiety, self-assertion, selfishness, greed, competition, and resentment.*

The first thing you will notice about a successful Avatar Master is that they are compassionate and real. This is no phony religion. You won't find Avatar Masters shuffling their feet, hat in hand, asking you for a donation. No. If they did, people would wonder how much to give. Did they give enough? Did they give too much? The whole transaction is surrounded with question marks. Masters just set a fair price and stick with it. They deliver a valuable service for a fair price.

Actually, it is better than a fair exchange, because the product does not wear out, and keeps getting better for the rest of the student's life. Don't you wish you could get a deal like that on a house or car, or even on a college education?

For me, and I think for many of the trainers here, it has been a long road from the sensory deprivation tank of 1986, up to now. We've dodged some of the worst people you can imagine, but also met many of the best and brightest.

I'm not sure how to express the deep appreciation that I have for your support and for your friendship. I think I'll just express my appreciation by continuing forward and contributing what I can to the creation of an enlightened planetary civilization. Feel free to join me if you like.

# THE STORY OF
# THE AVATAR MATERIALS

**Can Avatar help me with my relationship?**

Yes.

For most people relationships begin when they create mental impressions of each other. Without these mental impressions, they might not recognize each other.

Your mental impressions of other people are strongly colored by your own preferences, assumptions, and past. You take a sampling observation of the other, colored by the moment and event, add your conclusions, and then pull a costume from your closet and hang it on them.

*Will you be this costume for me?*

*Sure, if you will be this costume for me.*

Fred and Ginger, James and Moneypenny, or Mom and Dad, dance off together.

• *continues*

# The Story of
# The Avatar Materials
## • continued

The primary relationship is between you and your costume. These costumes are like adult dolls that you play with, fight with, and share your lives with. As long as the person assigned to the costume does not interrupt your game with actions out of character, things will go pretty much as you expect.

To go beyond your fantasy costume relationships, you must drop all of your mental representations of the other and meet them as a stranger/undefined being. This happens naturally on Section III of the Avatar Materials. Relationships are renewed on a more honest level.

By the way, you also can drop the mental representation you have of yourself and experience a liberating freedom.

Chapter 19

# The Beginning Of Avatar's Expansion

Six months after the first Avatars, we were invited to California to deliver the first West Coast Avatar class. There were supposed to be eleven people waiting to enroll in the class, but just before we arrived I learned that none had actually paid. All were waiting to hear me speak before they made their final decision. This was a surprise to me, because I had not prepared anything to say.

More surprises came at the airport. Our luggage was still in Pittsburgh, and the friend who picked us up told us that in addition to the eleven probable students, there were another fifty people waiting at his house to hear me speak. What am I going to say?

So, dirty, sweaty and tired, I found myself perched on a stool in a California living room with sixty strangers sitting on the floor around me. If the Avatar processes ever worked, they had to now. I closed my eyes and spent a minute handling my own doubts and nervousness. I applied the processes and the doubts slipped

away. When I opened my eyes, I floated in compassionate, undefined awareness. How are you my friends? Have I got a treat for you!

> I will try to describe Avatar without conveying too many of my own beliefs or perspectives to you. The reason I say that is because The Avatar Course is about your beliefs and your perspectives.

Absolute motionless silence! Sixty people, two babies and a dog, and you could hear the clock on the kitchen wall tick! It was so quiet that it finally unnerved the dog, and he surprised himself with a muffled bark. I felt I had said enough. They know. Let them feel me. Underneath the beliefs and body suits, we're part of this same awareness. Feel it.

The room relaxed as the fog of questions cleared. We had touched someplace behind it all and now were friends. We were in love. Eyes filled with tears. Gentle, accepting smiles. I love this feeling. We're real. The costumes are off and we're real. Together, for better or worse, part of a shared destiny.

> What you believe has consequences in your life. The Avatar course helps you to make the connection between what you are experiencing and the belief that is creating the experience.

> Imagine enrolling on a course where the study materials consist of your own consciousness. The teachers will provide navigational tools, a blank map, and emotional support. It's your exploration; you will bring your own terrain.

> Our purpose is to assist you in returning to the level of consciousness at which you are the knowing creative source of your own beliefs. Along the way you are going to learn that what you believe is not nearly as important as knowing

how you believe. In this case, understanding the container is more important than understanding the contents. Empty the contents. Marvel at the craft that creates the bowl.

Source Being is an effortless state of being. Don't confuse it with an attitude or identity that may be on automatic and seems effortless. Source Being is effortless, accepting and undefined. (Desiring and resisting are efforts. Accepting and appreciating are effortless.) From this state of being you can experience anything, and within extremely broad limits (perhaps boundless) change it as you decide.

This is the state of being that we call Avatar, and we have found a very simple and very effective procedure for achieving this state. It can be done in a matter of days when presented under the guidance of an experienced master. With the tools we teach you to use, you are equipped for the exploration of your own consciousness.

## Enlightenment or Your Money Back

Absolute motionless silence! Sixty people, two babies and a dog...

The Avatar Course is set up in three sections. Section I is for the intellect. It's food for thought. It requires only that you listen, read, or watch and, if you wish, contemplate what you have experienced. It is intended to bring about an understanding and a connection with a broader arena of life.

Then with the Section II materials, you start exploring—little expeditions into the backyard of your consciousness. Overnights! You practice the specific abilities and tools that are required to successfully manage what you are already experiencing in life. It's an opportunity to get your affairs in order before the big adventure begins.

Section II clarifies and expands an extrasensory perception channel to the physical universe that you may already be vaguely aware of—extended feeling. This is a non-sensory, non-emotional feeling that does not require physical contact. It quiets the mind and dramatically enhances your sense of being.

A hand went up in the audience. "Is it like meditation?"

Yes and no. It produces the same type of mental stillness that meditation produces, but it does so in a more interesting and much faster way. It's like meditation in that it is about gaining mastery of the mind—allowing the mind to still— but Avatar does it playfully without the struggle or confrontation. It's the difference between opening a safe by prying the door off or by using the combination. Avatar is the combination.

The group likes the analogy. Many of them have spent a lot of time prying.

Another exercise in Section II develops a skill in recognizing, creating, and changing judgments. This really begins to wake you up to the patterns in your life.

We experience what we experience in accordance with our judgments, which are the beliefs through which we filter our perceptions. Two people may experience the same event quite differently. For one of them it is traumatic and ruins their life; for the other it is inconsequential.

The difference is determined by the judgments the two people place on the experience.

The end result of this exercise is the ability to honestly relax judgment on anything being experienced. It lets you slip into your resisted experiences like entering a hot tub for a good soak. If you have been struggling with a body condition or a relationship, this exercise produces powerful realizations and turning-point experiences.

The final part of the Section II materials contains tools and exercises to remove barriers or blocks that you may have placed in front of your ability to create reality. We describe it as the most challenging experience anyone ever laughed through. It causes smile cramps in your face, increases your ability to create, and restores your control over existence.

In my mind I see the smiling faces of the students who have thanked me after completing this exercise. Their moist eyes occupy a special place in my memory. I also remember, somewhat sadly, the angry face of one student who didn't make it and denounced Avatar as a fraud. He was frozen at the controls of a failing life and couldn't let go of his righteous anger. Oh well, when it no longer serves him to be a victim, time will bring him back. Just a little more effort, a little more honesty, and he will make it too.

In case there were chronic victims present, I felt a little warning was in order.

If you are not completely satisfied with the results you achieve in Section II, don't go on to Section III. There's nothing in Section III that fixes poor results in Section II. If you don't go on and you decide within the next week or so that

Section II wasn't worth what you paid, I'll see to it personally that you get a refund check.

I smiled to myself. Has anyone ever offered enlightenment with a money-back guarantee?

## Avatar Is What You Are Looking For

A reporter who had been leaning against the kitchen door began to take notes.

*"The best way to bring out the goodness in others is to show it in yourself."*
*—Unknown*

So now, Section III, the main course. Section III begins with a guided initiation session conducted by an Avatar Master.

The initiation takes you on a tour of some of the most fundamental, transparent belief structures of consciousness—transparent because instead of seeing them, you see through them. The initiation experientially introduces you to procedures and tools that you can use to self-determinedly manage your life. Normally it is an insightful and enlightening experience that may leave you in a euphoric state for some time.

I would be surprised if they were not totally blissed out and euphoric for the rest of the day, but I didn't say that.

Following your initiation you will become an expert on the solo Avatar procedures. Now you are ready to explore. With the solo procedures and the occasional assistance of a trainer or fellow student, you begin your exploration with the Avatar rundowns. Each rundown addresses an area of experiences, beliefs, or attitudes that may be interfering with your appreciation of life. I'll go over the rundowns for you.

The first rundown is called Body Handle. The Body Handle processes produce effects similar to sensory deprivation tanking, but without the risk of isolation or panic reactions, and much more quickly. It assists you in recognizing the sensations and beliefs that keep you identified with a physical body and, if you choose, shows you how to function independently of a body. You experience yourself as a non-material spiritual being.

A couple in the front row looked at each other knowingly, and I realized they had just made the decision to sign up.

Body Handle also helps you to identify undesirable perceptions and sensations that you may have actually been installing in the body—the illusion is that they were coming from the body. The result of removing them is that the body is no longer held out of alignment by injurious beliefs or judgments.

Once you recognize and experience that you've been installing unpleasant sensations in the body, you can put back the sensations you wish to have. You may experience some remarkable healings.

A fascinating side effect of the Body Handle is the lucid or controlled dreaming that it produces. You learn to enter the dream state of consciousness without going to sleep. Some students have reported experiences of floating or flying and even assuming different bodies and exploring alternate dimensions. How would you like to spend an afternoon as a dolphin?

The second rundown is called Limitations. Have you ever explored any sort of spiritual or developmental path?

Most raised their hands.

Then you are aware that we set limitations on ourselves. We say, "I can't do this. I can't do that." And then we wonder why we can't do it.

Children's stories talk about the little steam engine that thought he could; the notion of positive thinking has been around for years. Well, this is a new look at the subject.

On the Limitations rundown, you eliminate specific limitations that interfere with the goals that excite you and bring you to life. You will probably not choose to handle all limitations, since some serve to focus your life.

*...you eliminate specific limitations that interfere with the goals that excite you and bring you to life.*

The third rundown is called Identities. Most people have a mental closet full of costumes that they carry around and project onto the people they meet. "Will you wear this costume for me?" "Will you be this person for me?"

When we get along well with people, it is generally because they are willing to wear the costume we offer them, and we are willing to wear one supplied by them.

Have you ever had someone put an identity on you that you didn't want to wear?

This brought nods of agreement from the group.

When you perceive another person without any costumes, judgments, or belief filters, you perceive them as a spiritual being. It is a profoundly moving experience to purely perceive another being without any distortion. It is a compassionate space that some have called unconditional love.

The fourth rundown is called Persistent Mass Handle. It gently guides you into the most resisted aspects of your life.

You can eliminate desires, compulsions, persistent pressures and pains that may have seemed beyond your control. The first sessions of Persistent Mass are done with another person acting as a facilitator. This is a very powerful process and produces amazing life-changing results.

The fifth and sixth rundowns are called respectively Universe Handle and Collective Consciousness Handle. You do these rundowns after you have resolved your own personal conflicts and wish to help the collective consciousness of life.

One of the ideas you create early in life is the idea of being someone. In fact, being someone is the experience of a belief. If you take awareness plus a belief about being someone and put them together, you get an individual. You can stay an individual by creating more beliefs that separate you further from collective consciousness—or with the Avatar procedures, you can eliminate the beliefs that cause separation, and experience a collective consciousness. You can change any beliefs you may have that separate you from pure creative awareness—the Aware Will.

In the Universe Handle rundown, you learn that all things are connected at some level of consciousness. In a sense, there is no individual consciousness, only segments of collective consciousness. With this exercise, you work on locating the limits that prevent you from joining the collective consciousness and operating within it.

*feeling* is *bringing what we are experiencing into this moment.*

> This obviously is a very high state of attainment, and students will vary in their ability and willingness to employ this technique.

> The last exercise is called The Ultimate Process. It is aptly named. It is guided by a coach.

> The whole course takes between seven and nine days, depending upon you.

I ended the talk by inviting people to reach out and feel me, not with their hands but with their awareness.

Everyone in the room seemed interested. I chatted with some friends and felt relief to see a line of students form in front of the registration table. The next day we began class with eighteen new students.

Within a few days the class grew so large with new arrivals that we had to move to a hotel, and our weeklong, 1987 West Coast delivery stretched into twelve weeks and several hundred students!

Old friends called each other with the message: "This is it! Come now!" One student arrived after hearing about Avatar from a phone call intended for his roommate. Another student received a psychic reading in which she was told to do Avatar. A third arrived because of a dream.

Because so many likened the experience of Avatar to waking up, they began to refer to themselves as Awakening Masters (AMs). Awakening Masters sent out a long-awaited wake-up call: "Avatar is what you are looking for."

Since 1987, tens of thousands of people from 72 different countries have completed their Avatar training.

*How do you conduct
yourself in the presence of
your own mind?*

*Do you sometimes
become lost, overwhelmed,
and blank?*

*Are you battered
by emotions?*

*Are you generally tolerant
and compassionate
rather than intolerant
and judgmental?*

*Are you engaged in a
struggle between deliberate
will and habitual mental
inertia?*

Chapter 20

# Shaking The YOU Out Of The Mind

Under the guidance of an Avatar Master, students can study and practice the use of the Avatar tools; learning discernment, identification, non-judgment, compassion, acceptance, and discreation. The purpose of these lessons is preparation for a solo-journey into the territory of their own minds. The Avatar Master does not burden (nor comfort) the students with beliefs. To do so would be to delay the students with obligations of worship, homage, or attachment. The Master gives practical training, builds confidence, and then stands aside.

The inward path begins somewhere after the initiation session in Section III of The Avatar Course. Students begin to discover their own unique mental patterns that they have been using to interpret perception. Most of these have been on autopilot. It is quite a remarkable discovery. Things that seemed senseless suddenly make sense.

*Real self is that which cannot be discreated, transcended or described.*

A separation between the being (real self) and the identities of the mind is realized. A private and personal door is opened through which the being can watch the mind without emotional response. Intentions, memories, and consequences that were shrouded in denial begin to show up.

The final instructions are on personal responsibility—free will choices. There are no maps and no footprints to follow. The time has arrived to stop reading, stop listening, and start watching, feeling, and shaping your own reality. Word lessons are replaced by world lessons. Some will find the experience awesome; some will find it fretful.

*According to the Hindu: If a man or woman fails to attain real self before casting off the body, they must again put on a body in the world of created things.*

Once the separation between real self and mind is stabilized, the real work of observing how your beliefs shape your life, and how they may be shaped, begins. The mind is complex. It is both conspicuous and subtle by turn; it operates across the instinctual, intellectual, and spiritual domains of life. Different states of mind have conflicting prime objectives. In its most conspicuous states the mind copies, reacts according to old conditioning, and reasons selfishly. In its subtle states it dreams, aspires, is altruistic, and is capable of experiencing extraordinary phenomena: ESP, intuition, precognition, etc. According to a Tibetan classic, the "Song of Milarepa," "The creations of the mind are more numerous than specks of dust in a ray of sunlight."

By itself, the mind is a causal system. One thing leads to another. One motivation is caused by an earlier motivation that was caused by an earlier motivation and so forth, back through time. Coming forward, one decision leads to another decision leads to another decision leads to where you are in life right now.

Something (a cause) makes something else happen (an effect). The impression left by the effect (new cause) makes something else happen (new effect). Consequence and motion stretch endlessly forward and backward from any event. This is mental inertia. Why am I afraid of cats (effect) traces back to being scratched. Why being scratched was such a trauma traces back to the look on Mama's face, which traces back to the look on her mama's face, which goes on back forever if you want to look.

*Some people are principally motivated by the effort to confirm what they believe about themselves.*

The discipline and concentration of following one of these chains of events back in time has some therapeutic value in terms of deliberate mind training, but looking for some basic cause that explains everything is a waste of time.

Minds would be as predictable, as predestined, and as unchanging as the laws of physics if it wasn't for one thing, YOU. This YOU, the real self, is not mind dependent. It can be awakened. This is the approach of Avatar.

Before you take on the world, you need to master your own mind. The foundation of Avatar training is learning how to create and maintain good relations with the various elements of your own mind. Living deliberately is both an art and a technology; it requires practice, patience, and tolerance.

*According to the Upanishad Veda: Above the senses is the mind; above the mind is the intellect (the fashioner of ideas and identities); above the intellect is the ego (I am, core identity); above the ego is the true self (undefined awareness, beingness that transcends any notion of itself, Source Being).*

## THE STORY OF
## THE AVATAR MATERIALS

### Will it work for me?

Most of the people who sign up with a Master for the Avatar training have the goal of improving their lives. Social connections and intellectual curiosity may be factors in their decision, but the tipping point is: "Will it work for me?"

This is not always a question that an Avatar Master can answer. Showing someone how to use a tool, even when the presentation includes many hours of drilling and exercises, will not always turn out a successful or motivated craftsman. Verifying that the tools work for others is still not an answer to, "Will it work for me?"

The real answer to this question is a question in reply, "What are you willing to change?"

Resisting is not letting something make an impression on you, experiencing is allowing something to make an impression on you. You have probably heard the legendary proverb, "What you resist persists." You also should hear, "When you DELIBERATELY experience what you are REALLY resisting, TRUE wisdom arises."

Chapter 21

# Let Us Not Speak Falsely

What is the greatest personal achievement? It is not any form of material wealth. It is not any quality of fame. It is not any degree of power. What then?

The greatest personal achievement is peace of mind.

Most people don't know much about peace of mind. They imagine that it is comfort, or leisure, a stress-free moment, maybe a restful night's sleep, but it is more than relief. Much more. Peace of mind is a quiet mental state that makes possible the experience of "just being." This is effortless awareness, undisturbed by thought or judgment, pain or pleasure, gain or loss.

Achieving peace of mind is the archetypal motive of human activity. Examine any school of principles and beliefs and you will discover that the ultimate aim of their instruction is (or was) to acquire peace of mind. There are many approaches to dealing with the mind: habituation, revelation, distraction, denial, submission, and subjugation, not to mention drugs, surgery, and shock treatments. Some succeed and some fail.

Those that succeed have acted as a reminder, as a key, or as a combination to a self-regulated force that was dormant within. The successful schools awaken and empower the being. (Many refer to this being as *spirit*.)

*"All that we are arises with our thoughts."*
*—Buddha*

The approaches that fail do so because they empower thinking and rely on methods of indoctrination and control—usually rewards and punishments. Often they promote activities that promise immediate pleasure but in time deliver stress, anxiety, addiction, and finally depression.

If the Avatar training has added anything to the canons of spiritual instruction and mind training, it is the discovery that certain deliberate combinations of mental processes (a shutdown procedure) result in peace of mind and open the door to an experience of spirit.

Consciousness has abilities that allow us to process and deal with the physical universe. Everyone is more or less aware of these abilities. Broadly they are imagining, thinking, and remembering. These are aspects of the mind.

Only a few people are aware that consciousness has a much broader, intrinsic nature above and beyond the mind. This intrinsic nature is the bridge to beingness. When it is entered, what was previously held to be important by imagining, thinking, and remembering is likely to become totally irrelevant. From this subtle realm, all of the events and experiences of normal waking consciousness are satisfactorily encompassed by the curiously wise expression, "That's something."

Assuming that people survive birth and fall within the normal parameters of genetic mutation, they are congenitally equipped with the thinking, imagining, and remembering types of conscious-ness—a mind. In truth, they are hardly equipped with anything else. The result is that the Being grows up with its attention focused on the rewards and difficulties of surviving in a defined physical reality. Celebration and struggle. Any hints that other realities exist (or could be created) that might offer more interesting games than variations of the pleasure-pain paradigm are relegated to fantasy or science fiction.

For most Beings the first real identity is a hastily constructed conscious definition: "I'm the baby." That is an anchoring affirmation in a meat body.

The sad part is that the Being spends the rest of its life at anchor. Its energy is spent patching and layering the original birthday affirmation with conclusions and experiences fashioned from perceptions of, and judgments about, physical reality.

It is a trap to confuse the realm of beingness with the physical universe.

Eventually, the Being arrives at the end of its physical-life days, still anchored in the definitions of the mind. You could call the mind the shallows of consciousness. What did the Being miss? The wonder of life? The awe of creation? The ecstasy of the Divine? Essentially, it missed any experience of deep awakening. Its only real experience is a sense of having been unhappily identified with a complex definition that required endless maintenance. This is what passes for a sane life in physical reality.

The Being departs the body and shakes off the amnesia of definitions. "Well," it says, "that's something," referring to the fading mental and decaying physical definitions that it dreamed was self. There is a belated recognition that thinking-imagining-remembering consciousness is severely limiting. It anchors life in one spot. So the Being gets the first lesson of Avatar, but without getting any of the tools. But it took a lifetime! That's way too slow. Can you imagine how many lifetimes it will take it to recognize that what it is experiencing may have something to do with what it is creating? Slow!

What is needed is a way for the Being to raise the anchor of self definitions, without dying, and set sail into the eternal realms beyond the mind. Getting back, going home. Exactly how to teach someone to do this has been the challenge of every spiritual practice. You see, the harder the Being works (imagines, thinks, remembers) to raise this anchor, the heavier the anchor grows. The mind can be an imprisoning paradox.

But wait. Now the Being sees all these Avatars sailing around having fantastic life adventures and still in touch with something more permanent than a paycheck. Intuitively the Being knows that the right to enlightenment and happiness is more than an accident of birth. The Being knows that there must be a way to slip the anchor of the mind.

How do you lift the anchor? The secret is to do nothing deliberately. How does a Being do nothing deliberately? That's a key world lesson. Without the Avatar tools, doing nothing deliberately is not easy to learn. It is a difficult experience to explain.

There are occasional moments in life when thinking stops and, among other things, a Being, becomes fully aware of the circumstances of its own physical incarnation without any reactions to it.

At least there ought to be such moments—periods of time when attention moves beyond the scope of daily concerns. The common self falls asleep, and an extraordinary self awakens. This extraordinary self, higher self, has a quality not found in the common self. That quality is the quiet mind viewpoint. Quiet mind is independent of time and does not react or create non-deliberately. The anchor of "I am this-not-that" disappears. Awareness awakens that is beyond any defining construction. This is truly a moment of enlightenment.

Achieving this state of quiet mind, even for a moment, is a profound accomplishment. An even greater accomplishment is maintaining this state. It is such an unusual accomplishment that when you tell a Being that the quiet mind state is an expected result of the Avatar training, you are usually met with disbelief.

The thinking-imagining-remembering mind is a restless creator. It rummages in the past for motives like a hungry bear in a pile of garbage. It projects intentions onto other people. It projects happiness and danger into the future. It creates imaginary scenarios, calculates and strategizes plans, vicariously predicts, and suffers consequences that never occur. It writes imaginary dialogs that are never spoken. It worries. It sings the same song over and over. It analyzes itself, scolding and praising according to some forgotten script. It frantically analyzes for hidden meaning in even the most innocent comment, ever explaining itself to itself.

Occasionally, somewhere between glee and despair, the Being wonders, "What is life all about?" And then it cautions itself to be realistic. It wonders some more about being quiet. "Quiet mind? Oh yes, I know quite a bit about that state. When I was in India...."

*If we only spoke the truth, there would be nothing to say.*

The quiet mind experience is so extraordinarily beautiful that many of the people who have momentarily experienced it spend the rest of their lives talking about it. This is how religions are born: Trying to describe an experience with a fundamental quality that is without description. This indescribable moment of experience becomes a sacred memory-shrine in the mind. Graven mental images! Still, it can be a beneficial memory in terms of coping with the stress and discouragement of life. It is a mental amulet of hope.

It is widely considered that the quiet mind experience can be reached only after long and hard practice (or perhaps temporarily induced by a shaman's magic). It is considered so fragile an experience that even a non-deliberate breath can shatter it. So it is quite a surprise that Avatar can teach a person how to deliberately produce this state in a matter of days. A pleasant surprise!

What is even more incredible, but probably true, is to realize that since Avatar's introduction in 1987, more Beings have stably achieved the state of quiet mind than in all of the ages before Avatar. It is no longer necessary to withdraw from the world, or live a life of self-denial, or risk your mental health to achieve a state of quiet mind. Just do Avatar.

Avatar Professional Course students, Orlando, FL, October 2010

Chapter 22

# Source Being:
# Deep Awakening

There are moments on The Avatar Course when all thought processes stop, and one becomes fully aware of existence without creating any reaction or response to it. Self moves beyond the scope of daily concerns, slips time and definition, and realizes itself as a facet of the description-less source in which all things, real or imagined, have their beginning. It is a moment of intuitive insight. An epiphany.

The Avatar student learns firsthand that no words or symbols will ever contain this state. And even though it is the source of description, it is itself always beyond description.

*Maybe the best way to explain Source is to describe the journey that leads to Source: Cease identifying with the physical body, cease identifying with mind, cease identifying with the self. What remains is Source Being.*

This is the transcendental experience, the divine ground. It turns the abstractions of philosophy into an experience that is profoundly more real than any other life event. It is a spiritual awakening. A wave of understanding is released that flows backward into the past and forward into the future of your life. The upsets and injustices of the past are soothed. The fears and anguish of the future fade back into the imagination. This is consecrated ground, the source from which all differences arise and to which all differences ultimately return. It is an eternal moment in which the seer and the seen, the knower and the known, share the same breath.

In this state there is no conflict with the interests of others, no struggle between opposites. With crystal clarity, you know both your own suffering and the suffering of the world as the result of the arbitrary structures of indoctrinated preferences and judgments. The illusion of separation vanishes. In all probability, your eyes will overflow with compassionate tears, and your heart will open to more love than you can imagine.

*Dropping definition and description begins the final leg of a being's spiritual journey.*

Attention-energy, once trapped in emotionally painful memories, returns to empower the senses to new thresholds of perception. Detail and beauty return to the world.

You realize that this state, which is far closer to your true essence than the labels you wear in ordinary existence, is always available to you. It is deeper than the changing qualities of the world. It prioritizes the importances of life. In all probability, you will have a good laugh.*

Buddhist scriptures have called this state of awareness nirvana. Hindu scriptures have called it Brahman. Christian scriptures have called it Christ consciousness. But the experienced Buddhist, Hindu, or Christian will all quickly tell you that nirvana, Brahman, or Christ consciousness are really just labels that point to an experience that cannot be described or conveyed by words.

So just relax and enjoy the experience.

Avatar students, who typically encounter this state in the third or fourth day of training, refer to the state as "source awareness." Presence replaces preconceived notions. Observation replaces judgments. Self-criticism and asserted rightness give way to a nonjudgmental, compassionate view of existence.

The value of Avatar (and the principle reason for its worldwide success) lies in the ability of a well-trained Avatar Master to lead a student through a custom-fitted series of practical exercises that unlock the suffering and struggle of restless mind, and open a path to a source awareness state of being.

*Deep awakening is giving up the effort to become something different or to experience something different.*

An Avatar Master is the key. The path is narrow and its sides slope steeply. The unguided seeker is more likely to fall into delusion or discouragement than he or she is to experience effortless Source Being. You can't see something while you are being it. You can't drive a car by looking at the road behind you. The great trap and whole nations have succumbed to this trap—is following the leaders and teachers, even those of good will, who preach out of the experience of delusion or discouragement. It is the world's misfortune that they didn't have an Avatar Master who really knew the path.

---

*\*While some people may liken this experience to descriptions of states induced by psychoactive drugs (e.g., LSD, mescaline, psilocybin) or yogic breathing exercises, it should be emphasized that Avatar does not employ either chemical or physical means to reach and sustain a transcendental state.*

# THE STORY OF THE AVATAR MATERIALS

*Are the results of Avatar permanent?*

That is up to you. Life is change. I don't think you would be happy with any state of mind or experience that never changed. Avatar is more about managing change than stopping it. The expected results of The Avatar Course are skills using a set of tools. Skills tend to last a long time. I can still ride a bike, still swim, and these are things that I learned long ago.

Chapter 23

# Why We Do This

Avatar is a set of tools that allows people, in a very short time, to identify and change the conclusions, decisions, and agreements that are shaping their lives. You could call it a mental editing technique, a belief management technique, or a spiritual empowerment technique. You could call it a lot of things, but the most important thing is that the tools work for you, and they work extremely well. People are amazed....

Avatar students systematically change their attitudes, remove self-imposed limitations, and end old hostilities that may be souring their experience of life. They set new goals or revive old ones, and using their rediscovered powers, create opportunities, motivation, and the courage to pursue dreams. In some cases, they restructure their own consciousness; in other cases they literally reshape physical reality. Yes, it is powerful stuff.

You could just stop reading now and do Avatar, and you wouldn't be sorry. But there is more to the story than personal development. There is something subtler that happens to you when you use the Avatar tools—a transformation takes place. For some, it happens in a matter of days; for others it takes considerably longer, even years.

The transformation takes one of two routes. The first route could be described as *satiation*. Satiation means to fully satisfy a desire.

When you are deliberately able to have, experience, or create the object of your desire, the result is not obsession or addiction; the result is satiation. That is a concept that is fully understood only after you become successful. How many chocolate-covered cherries can you eat? How long can you feel the best you've ever felt? How much money is enough? How much success is enough? (The joke answer is "a little more," but there really is a point of satiation.) When your personal desires are satiated you look for other ways in which to express your competence.

The second route of transformation begins when you become so skilled at self-examination that you begin to discover, deep within your mind, the conclusions, decisions, and agreements that are creating your desires. The enlightened insight is that with Avatar you can create or discreate anything you desire, including the **desire**.

This is the point where you begin to explore consciousness at a level beyond self-centered thinking. The self that you were being turns out to be a mental construct of conclusions, decisions, and agreements. A new self beyond mind awakens, right here, right now. You are now able to observe human consciousness from an exterior perspective. New possibilities appear. Values change. Awe and appreciation replace selfish desires. Compassion replaces antagonism. Cooperation replaces competition. Learning and social evolving replace intolerance.

*"Neither fire nor water, birth nor death, can erase our good deeds."*
*—Buddhist saying*

Ultimately you ask yourself the questions that every Being in the process of spiritual awakening asks, "What am I doing here? What is this really about? Why am I participating in this creation of life?"

And as an Avatar you know the answer—know it as a faint intuitive impulse that does not arise from forgotten mental indoctrination or identity ego-hunger. You are the answer, and are sustained by the realization that you have something to contribute to the creation of an enlightened planetary civilization; that is what you have always been about.

*The Avatar Materials are designed and intended to*
*be an effective means for inspiring the realizations and*
*changes that will move you toward a stable spiritual*
*awakening. They should be considered as means (tools),*
*rather than doctrines.*

Chapter 24

# Spiritual Paths

How do you achieve enlightenment?

Siddhartha Gautama lived in the forest, and then he moved to the city, lived there for a while, and then he moved to a mountain, lived there for a while, and then he moved to a river and lived beside the river for a while. Finally, under a banyan tree, he achieved a state of perfect enlightenment, and was henceforth called the Buddha.

So it seems to me that the path is pretty simple. First you live in the forest, then move to the city, then go live on a mountain, then live along a river, and then look for a banyan tree.

No? Then I guess it wasn't where Buddha was living that was important. What was important was that certain realizations and transformations were happening to him that culminated in his enlightenment. How does a spiritual path bring about these realizations and transformations leading to enlightenment?

Most spiritual paths employ various instructions, teaching techniques, rituals, and individual practices. Together these constitute the tools of a spiritual path. Some paths are more effective than others, and some paths are more personally suited to some mindsets than others. If a tool is used properly, it either produces the expected results or it doesn't. Of course, tools have other qualifying factors: ease of use, speed of result, effort involved, cost involved, and in some cases, avoidance of collateral damage.

The Avatar tools rate favorably in all categories and are remarkably effective considering the general mental condition of the people to which they are being introduced.

If you examine the current state of the world, you will find that most people are reacting according to deeply indoctrinated beliefs. Some will argue that they are not reacting and are making free will choices, but the truth is that past conclusions and old fears make most of their decisions. Nearly everyone is operating according to someone else's rules rather than their own intuitive principles. People live in what was, and they selectively perceive only enough of the present to excite their conclusions about things. The major aspiration is to be right rather than to be aware.

In this compulsive commerce of approval, most interactions are consciously or unconsciously manipulative. Most are governed by praise (pleasure) or criticism (pain). What people do and say to each other creates reactions. If the experience of the reaction is considered pleasurable, attachment develops. If the experience of the reactions is considered painful, resistance develops.

The same experience may affect different people differently. People's considerations of what is painful and what is pleasurable follow patterns created by their beliefs and memories of past experiences. If you traced the considerations of pain and pleasure all the way back to their roots, you would most likely find them associated with survival concerns: food, shelter, and reproduction.

At the present time, most of human consciousness operates like a roll of exposed film. It seldom pictures the world moment to moment as it is, but carries around pictures of what the world was like. Individuals wrestle with the tears and sufferings of the past—obstructions that rightly should be assigned to history and left there.

So this is where we begin.

The sections of Avatar are designed to encourage certain realizations and changes that a person must go through to move from a life of indoctrinated responses into a life of living deliberately. The necessary realizations and changes are not the same for everyone.

*As soon as the definitionless Source becomes comfortable being a definitionless Source, identification with a defined self becomes a matter of choice.*

Also, the realizations and changes are not a straight line or an exact series of steps. Instead, they follow a winding path of necessarily unique experiences that sometimes nurture the ego self, sometimes a compassionate self, and slowly or suddenly, arrive at an experience of spiritual self. It may sound like a linear process, but it seldom is.

Word lessons can be presented as a straight path to understanding enlightenment, chapter following chapter, but world lessons wander; life stops to explore. It loses its place. It falls down, runs into walls, sheds tears, and then has a good laugh as it gets up and brushes itself off. If only perfect people could experience enlightenment, very few would arrive.

Progress does not always mean that you are moving in the direction of being more compassionate, righteous, or spiritual. The unique experience you need might be painful or destructive. Sometimes the next lesson is negative, or ego strengthening, or overwhelming. Unless you are able to live a cloister-like life, your spiritual tools need to work on practical matters as well as metaphysical matters.

As an aside, religions tend to stall out around the high points of a spiritual path. These hesitations can be obstructions to moving forward. Sometimes a parishioner has to fall into sin and be excommunicated before he or she can move on. The last step before personal freedom may be to commit an unpardonable sin in your faith. The transgressions, honestly confronted, transform your judgments into compassion and empathy for others. Someone who always acts kindly has trouble understanding someone who fails to act kindly. Not doing good might seem unforgivable to someone who always does good.

I am going to take you through the sections of Avatar one by one and roughly describe the changes that are expected to occur in each section. But let me caution you, reading about these changes, even in detail, is not the same as experiencing them.

Section I of the Avatar Materials is called ReSurfacing. It refers to the action of disentangling you from your creations; it is an awakening of interested

self-awareness. This section could be called a self-discovery course. It is waking you up from the movie you were lost in.

ReSurfacing reminds people that there is a difference between the experience of self and the experience the self is having. Later on the path, these two may again merge, but at this level of awakening the direction is to realize that there is a difference between the perceiver and the perception. There is a difference between one's self and one's role model. There is a difference between acting deliberately and reacting. There is a difference between you and your problems.

The fundamental change that occurs on ReSurfacing is a deepening of the experience of "I am."

This is a transformation from, "Oh sure, I am," to "Oh my God, I am. I really am." This is an "I am" that is discovering personal responsibility. This opens the door to powerful realizations that break the grip of indoctrinated beliefs. Experiencing "I am" as something more than a mental concept causes a transformation and a healing. Personal responsibility replaces robotic reactions to authority. Suddenly you can observe and choose how, or even if, you will act. When somebody talks about Avatar as a self-discovery course, they're talking about this level of realization and change.

Section II of Avatar is self-empowerment training. The prerequisite to doing Section II is that during ReSurfacing you discovered a real self to empower.

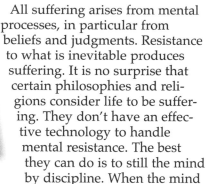

All suffering arises from mental processes, in particular from beliefs and judgments. Resistance to what is inevitable produces suffering. It is no surprise that certain philosophies and religions consider life to be suffering. They don't have an effective technology to handle mental resistance. The best they can do is to still the mind by discipline. When the mind is still, the suffering ceases, but so too do the lessons conveyed by suffering.

Section II is a modern approach to achieving control over the mind. There is more subtleness to the mind than turning it off and on. This control is such an unusual accomplishment that many people, until they experience it, do not believe it can be done. But it can, and it is part of the changes that happen on Section II of Avatar.

After you sort out who you are and how your mind operates, the next issue is what can you deliberately create?

Section II is where the path begins to wind. You might take a detour into the material world. Ego development is built into the exercises in order to prepare for the next transformation. After the experience of "I am," the next experience on the path is, "And I'm pretty darned cool." Section II removes your limitations and releases your creative powers. Your first response will probably be to create something that you have long desired. This is the ultimate pleasure of the ego, to create exactly what one wants.

Why, you might ask, would Avatar encourage the development of the ego when we know the ego is the source of many difficulties in the world? The answer is that it is the next necessary experience that you need to integrate. The ego is an area that needs to be explored without judgment. Remember, sometimes it is the egotistic efforts at self-aggrandizement that produce some of our greatest cultural treasures. Developing the ego is a necessary rite of passage to transcending the ego. If your ego fails to flower, there is no harvest, and no further spiritual growth.

*Whether you'll be happy or not when you get what you want depends upon the conduct you followed while getting what you want.*

The main change on Section II is achieving a balance in your life. If you have experienced unhappiness, you can create happiness. If you have experienced failure, you can experience success. If you have experienced feeling submissive, you can balance it with feeling dominant. The Section II Source List processes and Reality Creation processes afford an ethical way for you to achieve this balance.

Restoring balance is the real goal of self-empowerment. You could say that Section II puts you on the route to achieving karmic balance with the universe; whatever twists and turns your spiritual path has taken, or needs to take, the balance can be restored with the Section II tools.

On to Section III. The first rays of self-awareness are often paralyzing; they tend to brightly illuminate your shame and guilt, rather than your deeper nature. This changes with the initiation of Section III; self-awareness becomes functional, compassionate, and empowering.

The Section III rundowns are a journey inward to unlimited self. They bring you into the space that has the power to define self. The rundowns identify and release the tentacles of the past, and you come effortlessly into a deep level of the present. The present rather than the past now shapes who you are and what you choose to experience. In this state, you act intuitively, are motivated by high principles, and operate from an awareness that is independent of self.

So these are the sections that make up The Avatar Course. They are intended to be experiential rather than intellectual.

I hope you have had some realizations from reading this book; I hope you do Avatar, but even if you don't, may you be happy and well.

Sending you fearless love,
Harry Palmer

# Epilogue

We will not achieve an Enlightened Planetary Civilization in the tomorrow that arrives next month, or in the tomorrow that arrive next year, or maybe not even in any of the tomorrows of our lifetime, but there will be a tomorrow when we do arrive. That is what you will remember from this moment in time, what you will tell your children and grand children; humanity will evolve into an enlightened planetary civilization. It is possible, and that is the direction in which we are headed. We have passed the tipping point where the creation of an Enlightened Planetary Civilization has evolved from one man's fantasy to an ideal held by a social movement.

One of the earliest groups in the human potential movement was the Free Masons. Among their many rituals were instructions for closing a lodge meeting. I think those instructions are appropriate here.

*"We are now about to quit this sacred retreat of friendship and virtue to mix again with the world. Amidst its concerns and employment forget not the duties that you have heard so frequently inculcated, and so forcibly recommended in this lodge. Remember, that around this altar, you have promised to befriend and relieve every brother (and sister) who shall need your assistance. You have promised in the friendliest manner to remind him (or her) of his (or her) errors and aid a reformation. These generous principles are to extend further: Every human being has a claim upon your kind offices. Do good unto all... be ye all of one mind, live in peace, and may the God of love and peace delight to dwell with you and bless you."*

# The Avatar Materials

| The Avatar Course | Course requirements | Available from | Teaches about |
| --- | --- | --- | --- |
| Section I The ReSurfacing Workshop | None | Any Avatar Master currently licensed to deliver The Avatar Course. | Preliminary course information. Philosophical principles of Avatar. Exercises to produce insight and connection with higher levels of consciousness. |
| Section II The Exercises | A familiarity with *ReSurfacing*. | Any Avatar Master currently licensed to deliver The Avatar Course. | The principles governing creation and experience. Exercises to enhance the perception of creation and to restore the ability to create reality. |
| Section III The Procedures | Recovery of the experience of your own sourceness. | Any Avatar Master currently licensed to deliver The Avatar Course. | The principles governing discreation and the management of reality. Personal initiation and seven solo rundowns that handle aspects of existence. |

| The Avatar Master Course | Course requirements | Available from | Teaches about |
| --- | --- | --- | --- |
| Section IV (a) Awakening | Completion of The Avatar Course and an invitation from your Avatar Master. | Delivered only by Star's Edge delivery teams. | Source Beingness. The structure and mechanics of personal identity. Locating core beliefs. Shifting perspective. Instructions on delivering initiation sessions and supervising rundowns. |
| Section IV (b) The Professional Course: Beyond Awakening | Completion of Section IV (a) of The Avatar Master Course. | Delivered only by Star's Edge delivery teams. | The components of life: Beingness, Motivation, Perception, Operation, Organization, Alignment. Using attention to create without becoming trapped by it. |

| The Avatar Wizard Course | Course requirements | Available from | Teaches about |
| --- | --- | --- | --- |
| Section V Extrasensory abilities | Completion of Section IV (a) of The Avatar Master Course. | Delivered only by Star's Edge International. | The collective consciousness. Levels and abilities of consciousness. Hidden influences on life. Leadership and civilization management. |

| Expected results | Cost/time |
|---|---|
| Greater connection with and insight into the nature of personal reality. The ability to discover your most secret beliefs. | US $295<br>2 days |
| The ability to perceive reality without judgments, distortion, or separation; to modify personal reality; to create experientially real states of beingness at will. | US $500<br>4 to 5 days |
| The ability to address body sensations, interpersonal conflicts, dependencies, self-sabotaging beliefs, and compulsions; to assume full responsibility for the conditions and circumstances of your own life. | US $1500<br>2 to 4 days |

| Expected results | Cost/time |
|---|---|
| The ability to handle persistent conditions and a certainty on the workability of the Avatar Materials. Successful graduates receive a provisional license as assistants, interns or fully licensed Avatar Masters, to organize and participate in Avatar deliveries that exceed student expectations. | US $3000<br>9 days |
| An understanding of the purpose of life and the ability to remain comfortably present in difficult circumstances. | US $2500<br>7 days |

| Expected results | Cost/time |
|---|---|
| The ability to understand and manage creation. The ability to operate from the viewpoint of the higher self. The ability to transform civilization. | US $7500<br>13 days |

# Alignment

*When you are ready to explore
the deeper workings of your
own consciousness and become
familiar with the creation that
you regard as self....*

$15.00 USD

# Living Deliberately

## The Discovery and Development of Avatar

In 1987, Harry outlined an intriguing series of mental procedures. When correctly applied, these procedures unravel many of the more profound mysteries of human consciousness. This book chronicles the discovery and development of Avatar and sets the stage for students taking The Avatar Course.

$15.00 USD

# ReSurfacing®

## Techniques for Exploring Consciousness

### *Who am I?   Why am I here?   Where am I going?*

ReSurfacing refers to the action of disentangling yourself from old creations and rising back into awareness. The ReSurfacing workbook is a guide for exploring the inner workings of your own consciousness.

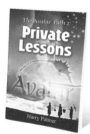

$21.95 USD

# The Avatar Path 2:

## Private Lessons

Private Lessons are extrapolated from the advanced Avatar Materials. They are intended to be contemplative slices of subjects rather than full explanations. The sequence is subtle to non-existent. Some slices belong together, for example, the sections on creative study, domains of being, and relationships. Other slices are single pieces that you will have to stitch to the whole.

# What Is Avatar?

**The Avatar Course** is a powerful and speedily effective course based on the simple truth that your beliefs will cause you to create or attract situations and events that you experience as your life.

**The Goal** of the three-section course is to guide you in an exploration of your own belief system and to equip you with the tools to modify those things that you wish to change. The Avatar Course opens a window to the inner workings of your own consciousness.

**The Course** teaches world lessons (experiential) rather than word lessons (intellectual). For this reason it requires a trained AVATAR MASTER to guide you into the actual lessons already contained in your own consciousness.

*Avatar teaches the use of proven navigational tools that can be used, in harmony with your own integrity, to pass safely across the uncharted turbulence of the mind into the region of the soul.*
*—Harry Palmer*

## The Free Avatar Information Pack

What Is Avatar? • Avatar: Practical & Mystical
• Ten Actions You Can Do Today To Start Taking Back Your Life • *Special Gift:* An Avatar Compassion Card

Get your free Avatar Information pack today by visiting **www.TheAvatarCourse.com/info** or call the number below.

## To Order

*Call 800-589-3767, contact your local Avatar Master, or visit www.AvatarBookstore.com.*

# More From Harry Palmer

**3 Paths Of Avatar** DVD *Three talks on one DVD*
(12 subtitled languages) $49.95

**Personal Responsibility, Compassion, & Service To Others** DVD
(12 subtitled languages) $19.95

**How To Explain Everything** DVD
(12 subtitled languages) $19.95

**Impressions** DVD
(16 subtitled languages) $19.95

**Don't Sell Yourself Short** DVD
(11 subtitled languages) $19.95

**Managing Change** DVD
(15 subtitled languages) $19.95

**It's Getting Better** DVD
(15 subtitled languages) $19.95

**Source Beingness** DVD
(14 subtitled languages) $19.95

**Make Up Your Mind** DVD
(17 subtitled languages) $19.95

**Everything Is Alright** DVD
(13 subtitled languages) $19.95

**Bottled Consciousness** DVD $12.95

**Make The Best Of What Happens Next** DVD $12.95

Life Challenges DVD
(14 subtitled languages) $19.95

Stay Awake And Relax DVD $12.95

Connection & Encouragement DVD $12.95

Three Questions Of Enlightenment CD $6.95

1987 West Coast Tour: *Welcome To Avatar* CD $6.95

How To Create Magic In Your Life CD $6.95

Love Precious Humanity®:
*The Collected Wisdom of Harry Palmer* book $19.95

Seven Pillars of Enlightenment: *The Avatar Mini-Courses* book $35.00

Inside Avatar The Book:
*Achieving Enlightenment* book $12.95

Thoughtstorm Manual®: *An Evolution In Human Thinking* $15.95

The Avatar Master's Handbook $24.95

Awaken: *The Avatar Diaries* $5.00

## To Order

*Call 800-589-3767, contact your local Avatar Master, or visit www.AvatarBookstore.com.*

# Avatar Online

## TheAvatarTimes.com

*Explore and understand the relationship between your beliefs and your experiences.*

Avatar closes forever the overdue accounts of past mental therapies and religious ideologies and confirms the creative potential of the human spirit. These are the Avatar Times. Visit this website to subscribe to the FREE Avatar Times Newsletter.

This site is translated into many different languages.

## TheAvatarCourse.com

Your Source to Explore the Most Powerful Self-Development Program Available

Want to know more about the Avatar path? This website is the place to start. You can download articles by Harry, watch Avatar videos, sign up for the free Avatar Times newsletters, connect with a local Avatar Master, and more.

## AvatarResults.com

Personal Stories & Insights from Avatar Students

After every course Star's Edge receives many letters where Avatar students share their insights, love, thanks, gratitude and support.

A small fraction of the more than 500,000 letters that Star's Edge has received from our students are available on this website.

## AvatarJournal.com

Insights & Tools for the Expansion of Consciousness

*The Avatar Journal* is a free online publication featuring news and articles from all over the Avatar world. Visit for the good news.

# AvatarBookstore.com

## The Place for Avatar Publications and Products

Want a copy of "Living Deliberately"? Are you looking for Harry's "Life Challenges" talk on DVD? This is the site for Avatar publications and products.

# AvatarEPC.com

## Contributing to the Creation of an Enlightened Planetary Civilization

On this site you'll find information about Star's Edge International, the company that oversees the Avatar courses, as well as links to other Avatar websites.

# EarthsCompassionTeam.com

## Supporting Compassionate Leadership Worldwide

Supporting leaders to consistently take action through compassion is imperative in our rapidly evolving world. This website is dedicated to that goal.

Together we can change what was into what could be!

www.facebook.com/AvatarCourse
www.facebook.com/CompassionProject
www.facebook.com/TheAvatarPath
www.twitter.com/AvatarCourse

# Avatar

Would you like to be free of old restraints that make you unhappy?

Would you like to align your beliefs with the goals you want to accomplish?

Would you like to feel more secure about your ability to conduct your own life?

Would you like to experience a higher, wiser, more peaceful expression of self?

Would you like to be able to rise above the sorrows and struggles of the world and see them for what they really are?

Would you like to experience the state of consciousness traditionally described as enlightenment?

Avatar is for you.

Would you like to know more about yourself and the world you live in? Would you like to explore more deeply the creation you regard as self? Then have an Avatar Master contact you. With thousands of Avatar Masters all over the world there is sure to be one close by. Send your name, address, and telephone number to:

Star's Edge International
237 N Westmonte Dr
Altamonte Springs, FL 32714 USA

tel: 407-788-3090 or 800-589-3767
fax: 407-788-1052
e-mail: avatar@avatarhq.com
website: www.AvatarEPC.com

*Let us know the best time and method to contact you and we will have a licensed Avatar Master get in touch with you.*